D0937437

C. S. LEWIS FOR THE
THIRD MILLENNIUM

PETER KREEFT

C. S. Lewis for the Third Millennium

Six Essays on *The Abolition of Man*

IGNATIUS PRESS   SAN FRANCISCO

Cover by Roxanne Mei Lum

© 1994 Ignatius Press, San Francisco
All rights reserved
ISBN 0–89870–523–1
Library of Congress catalogue number 94–75995
Printed in the United States of America

FOR WALTER HOOPER
WITH GRATITUDE
FOR GIVING THE WORLD
MANY OF LEWIS' PRECIOUS WRITINGS
AND MUCH OF LEWIS' GRACIOUS SPIRIT

CONTENTS

INTRODUCTION

As our senile, toothless, and confused culture stumbles blindly
toward the third millennium; as our "century of genocide" comes
to an end, having murdered more human beings (born and unborn)
in a single century than the total of all men who lived in all
previous centuries; as our demonic "culture of death" accelerates
its sharklike feeding frenzy of human bodies *and souls;* and as our
arrogant and impenitent planet rushes naked and defenseless through
space and time on a collision course with the fearsome heavenly
body of the justice of God, we wonder: "What next?"—and even
whether there will *be* a "next". We look for prophets.

I believe the two most prophetic books of our century are
Aldous Huxley's *Brave New World* and C. S. Lewis' *Abolition of
Man.* If you want to see the third millennium, read these two
books.

Lewis has one great advantage over Huxley: he is a Christian.
Therefore he holds out hope, appeals to moral choice, and offers a
positive alternative, though his jeremiad is no less horrific than
Huxley's scenario of doom. But the hope, the alternative, and the
choice are not limited to Christians. The spiritual war of this
century is not among different religions but between all religions
and none. That is why what is happening in Bosnia and Northern
Ireland is not merely wicked, it is hopelessly out-of-date: a civil
war breaking out in the ranks during a global and apocalyptic war
against Hell. *The Abolition of Man* appeals to all men of good will
and sound mind. So does this book: six essays about *The Abolition
of Man* applied to our time and our future.

The first essay, "How to Save Western Civilization: C. S. Lewis as Prophet", summarizes Lewis' philosophy of history.

The second, "Darkness at Noon: The Eclipse of 'The Permanent Things'", summarizes our era from the standpoint of this philosophy.

The third, "The Goodness of Goodness and the Badness of Badness", is a defense of the Natural Law, or objective values as the absolute *sine qua non* for the survival of civilization, and a summary of Lewis' refutation of twenty alternatives to it.

The fourth, "Can the Natural Law Ever Be Abolished from the Heart of Man?", puts Lewis in dialogue with Saint Thomas Aquinas on whether the abolition of man (i.e., man as moral) can ever happen.

The fifth, "Walker Percy's *Lost in the Cosmos: The Abolition of Man* in Late-Night Comedy Format", is some comic relief on the same heavy topics treated in chapters 1 through 4.

And the sixth, "The Joyful Cosmology: *Perelandra's* 'Great Dance' as an Alternative World View to Modern Reductionism", fleshes out Lewis' hopeful conclusion in *The Abolition of Man*: a new and humane world view or cosmology that is the necessary background for the new life view or morality. The newness is a restoration of the old. When radicalism is the establishment, the only really radical revolution is traditionalism.

The six essays are literally "essays", explorations—into the single most momentous question of our desperate times. I invite the reader to join me on my six little rafts following in the wake of Lewis' pioneering ship to explore the whirlpools and rapids of this great, roaring river that is our common culture, now apparently headed for the falls. Whether and how it is possible to avert this fate is one of the few really relevant things to think about today.

How to Save Western Civilization: C. S. Lewis as Prophet

Cars have windshields as well as rearview mirrors. So do civilizations. However, our rearward, Epimethean vision is far stronger than our forward, Promethean one. We have more archivists than prophets. For archivists see through a microscope, sharply, but prophets see through a glass, darkly.

Yet even the little the prophets see is of great importance to us. It is like the little but all-important view that a driver sees when peering through a tiny hole of light in a muddy windshield when the car is accelerating through thick fog over rocks and between abysses—in other words, when the situation is like that of our civilization.

The gift of prophecy, confined to a small number in Old Testament times, was offered to all Christians once the Holy Spirit, the One who makes and inspires prophets, was spread through the Church and into the world in the New Covenant. It is possible therefore without absurdity to call C. S. Lewis a prophet. Let us consult the writings of this most popular Christian author of our age with that hope in mind and look for some Lewis-light

This chapter originally appeared in *A Christian for All Christians*, edited by Andrew Walker and James Patrick (London: Hodder and Stoughton, 1990).

on our civilizational teeter, we who stand poised on the brink of spiritual suicide.

I extract twelve major principles about history from Lewis: five could be called a philosophy of history, four a description of history, and three a psychology of history. Then I apply these twelve principles to the issue of the future of mankind on this planet and draw a single conclusion from them. Finally, from this conclusion I derive a number of immediately practical applications for our present lives.

The first and most important principle of Lewis' philosophy of history is that he disbelieves in the philosophy of history. In his Cambridge inaugural lecture "De Descriptione Temporum", he said:

> About everything that could be called 'the philosophy of history' I am a desperate skeptic. I know nothing of the future, not even whether there will be any future. . . . I don't know whether the human tragi-comedy is now in Act I or Act V, whether our present disorders are those of infancy or old age.

In his volume on the sixteenth century in the *Oxford History of English Literature,* he wrote:

> Some think it is the historian's business to penetrate beyond this apparent confusion and heterogeneity and to grasp in a simple intuition the 'spirit' or 'meaning' of his period. With some hesitation, and with much respect for the great men who have thought otherwise, I submit that this is exactly what we must refrain from doing. I cannot convince myself that such 'spirits' or 'meanings' have much more reality than the pictures we see in the fire. . . . The 'canals' on Mars vanished when we got stronger lenses.

And any reader of the above volume knows that Lewis has strong lenses.

Finally, from *Reflections on the Psalms,* here is the *reason* for Lewis' skepticism about the philosophy of history:

Between different ages there is no impartial judge on earth, for no one stands outside the historical process; and, of course, no one is so completely enslaved to it as those who take our own age to be not one more period but a final and permanent platform from which we can see all other ages objectively.

The Christian religion is like the history of the human race: messy, unpredictable, surprising, and lacking "suspicious a priori lucidity", as Lewis puts it in *Miracles:*

> Christianity, faced with popular 'religion,' is continually trouble-some . . . the real historian is similarly a nuisance when we want to romance about 'the old days' or 'the ancient Greeks and Romans.' The ascertained nature of any real thing is always at first a nuisance to our natural fantasies.

"Don't confuse me with facts; I've made up my mind" is a far more prevalent attitude than we like to think.

But once we give up fantasizing about history, we need not give up talking about it. Although our first Lewisian principle about the philosophy of history seems to exclude any further principles, it does not. It excludes only firm generalizations, dogmatic conclusions. Principles are not conclusions but starting points, *principia*. When we *start* to approach history, we need principles as one of the two blades of our mental scissors, if they are to cut through the mass of historical paper. We also need a lower, empirical blade, lest we project our a priori principles onto the facts. Principles without facts are empty, but facts without principles are blind.

Principle Two could be called anti-historicism, or perhaps anti-Hegelianism. Before Hegel, nearly everyone agreed that Truth, could we but know it, must be unchanging — at least truths about human nature and the laws of good and evil. Truths about our accidental qualities may change through history, but the laws of our essence can never change. As Lewis put it in *A Preface to*

'*Paradise Lost*', "Though the human heart is not unchanging (nay, changes in the twinkling of an eye), the laws of causation are. When poisons become fashionable they do not cease to kill."

Modern man, therefore, continues to make the same essential mistakes, is subject to the same addictions, sins the same sins, and reaps the same whirlwinds as his ancestors. The only essential changes in the human condition were the Fall and the Redemption. Nothing will ever change our very nature. No Superman looms on the horizon. The "rough beast" has already slouched toward Bethlehem to be born; there will be no others (except false messiahs) until the end of time.

That is why Lewis is continually turning us from our search for "contemporary relevance" to eternal relevance, as in this quotation from *A Preface to 'Paradise Lost'*:

> The crisis of the present moment, like the nearest telegraph pole, will always loom largest. Isn't there a danger that our great, permanent, objective necessities—often more important—may get crowded out?
>
> While the moderns have been pressing forward to conquer new territories of consciousness, the old territory, in which alone man can live, has been left unguarded, and we are in danger of finding the enemy in our rear.

On the first page of *The Allegory of Love,* Lewis gives the reason in principle why the study of the past is just as useful for an understanding of ourselves and our nature as a study of the present: "Humanity does not pass through phases as a train passes through stations; being alive, it has the privilege of always moving yet never leaving anything behind. Whatever we have been, in some sort we are still." And from Letter no. 146, written in 1931: "I find nothing obsolete. The silly things the great men say were as silly then as they are now; the wise ones are as wise now as they were then."

Supposedly new fundamental ideas nearly always turn out to be old. Even technology is only sober and successful magic. The dream of "man's conquest of nature" is only Prometheus and Faust secularized. Modernist theology is only the new Arianism. Determinism is only the new astrology. Kantianism is only the new Sophism in epistemology and the new Stoicism in ethics. The list is endless. The only radically new thing under the sun is the one Man who came from beyond the sun.

Principle Three is a negative one: a decisive disagreement with the prevailing philosophy of history, Progressivism or Universal Evolutionism. Principle Two denied *essential* change in the human species; Principle Three denies accidental change for the better in the last few centuries—something which, unlike essential change, *could* have happened but didn't, according to Lewis. Like a rock standing against the popular stream of progressivism, Lewis refused to idealize the twentieth century. I think he would understand the vision of Pope Leo XIII in which God gave the devil one century to do his worst work in, and the devil chose the twentieth.

Lewis loves to attack the cult of change for the sake of change, the exaltation of change and the demeaning of permanence, and the usual rhetoric that goes with it. He asks, in *"De Descriptione Temporum"*,

> How has it come about that we use the highly emotive word 'stagnation' with all its malodorous and malarial overtones for what other ages would have called 'permanence'? Why does the word 'primitive' at once suggest to us clumsiness, inefficiency, barbarity? Where our ancestors talked of the primitive church or the primitive purity of our condition, they meant nothing [pejorative].

His answer to the above question is found in the same lecture, given at Cambridge:

> I submit that what has imposed this climate of opinion so firmly on the human mind is a new archetypal image. It is the

image of old machines being superseded by new and better ones. For in the world of machines the new most often really is better and the primitive really is clumsy. . . .

Our assumption that everything is provisional and soon to be superseded, that the attainment of goods we have never yet had, rather than the defence and conservation of those we have already, is the cardinal business of life, would most shock and bewilder [our ancestors].

Reason cuts through the fog of rhetoric to refute this myth:

Let us strip it of the illegitimate emotional power it derives from the word 'stagnation' with its suggestion of puddles and mantled pools. If water stands too long it stinks. To infer thence that whatever stands long must be unwholesome is to be the victim of metaphor. Space does not stink because it has preserved its three dimensions from the beginning. The square on the hypotenuse has not gone mouldy by continuing to equal the sum of the squares on the other two sides. Love is not dishonoured by constancy. . . .

The last point is the crucial one. It is in ethics that "progressivism" is most deadly. Astonishingly, few modern minds see the simple and obvious point that an unchanging standard, far from being the enemy of moral progress, is the necessary condition for it: "Does a permanent moral standard preclude progress? On the contrary, except on the supposition of a changeless standard, progress is impossible . . . if the terminus is as mobile as the train, how can the train progress toward it?"

Lewis' Christianity gives him a much more radically progressive outlook than evolutionism can give, for Christianity calls on men to become not just better men or even Supermen but to become Christs, to share in divine life—an infinitely greater transformation than any current secular fad.

Christian prophets, like Christ, are the true progressives, but not in the way of current Liberalism, by "keeping up with the world". Lewis writes,

It sounds well to say that the true prophet is a revolutionary, going further and faster than the forward movement of the age, but the dictum bears little relation to experience. The prophets have *resisted* the current of their times.... [I]t would require a more than common effrontery of paradox to present Jeremiah as the nose on the face of the Zeitgeist.

Lewis knew that in every field progress is made only by those who ignore the Zeitgeist and simply tell the truth. Thus he says in *The Problem of Pain:* "I take a very low view of 'climates of opinion.' In his own subject every man knows that all discoveries are made and all errors corrected by those who ignore the 'climates of opinion.'"

Lewis gives a brilliant description in *The Discarded Image* of the "evolution revolution", the revolutionary change the evolutionary world view has effected:

In modernism, i.e., in evolutionary thought, man stands at the top of a stair whose foot is lost in obscurity; in [medieval thought]...he stands at the bottom of a stair whose top is invisible with light.

That all perfect things are prior to all imperfect things was common ground to nearly all ancient and medieval thinkers except the Epicureans.... [T]he radical difference which this involves between their thought and the developmental or evolutionary concepts of our own period . . . leaves no area and no level of consciousness unaffected.

Lewis' reason for rejecting the myth of universal progress is essentially Chesterton's observation that Universal Evolutionism seems credible only when you blink one eye; when you remember the fact that oaks come from acorns and forget the fact that acorns come from oaks; when you remember that big New York grew from little New Amsterdam and forget that little New Amsterdam came from big, old Amsterdam; when you remember that jumbo jets came from the Wright brothers' little flying toy but forget that the Wright brothers' little toy came from the Wright brothers' highly complex brains.

Lewis' Principle Four is another denial: the denial of the corollary of Evolutionary Progressivism that Lewis labels "chronological snobbery" and defines in *Surprised by Joy* as "the uncritical acceptance of the intellectual climate common to all our age and the assumption that whatever has gone out of date is on that account dated". Reason erects a stop sign to this prejudice:

> You must find out why it went out of date. Was it ever refuted (and if so by whom, where and how conclusively) or did it merely die away as fashions do? If the latter, this tells us nothing about its truth or falsehood. From seeing this, one passes on to the realization that our own age is also 'a period,' and certainly has, like all periods, its own characteristic illusions. They are likeliest to lurk in those widespread assumptions which are so ingrained in the age that no one dares to attack or feels it necessary to defend them.

(Lewis gives Owen Barfield credit for teaching him this all-important principle.)

In his essay "Historicism", Lewis calls chronological snobbery "the vulgarest of all vulgar errors, that of idolizing as the goddess History what manlier ages belaboured as the strumpet Fortune".

"Chronological snobbery" is self-defeating, for "the more 'up-to-date' the look is, the sooner it will be dated." In *An Experiment in Criticism,* Lewis asks the avant-garde critic, "If you take your stand on the 'prevalent' view, how long do you suppose it will prevail? . . . All you can really say about my taste is that it is old-fashioned; yours will soon be the same."

Lewis freely confesses in a letter (no. 179, 1940) that "In talking to me you must beware because I am conscious of a partly pathological hostility to what is fashionable." He speaks of himself as "a converted Pagan living among apostate Puritans" and says (in *Surprised by Joy*), "The key to my books is Donne's maxim, 'the heresies that men leave are hated most.' The things I assert most vigorously are those that I resisted long and accepted late."

Alan Watts finds in Lewis "a certain ill-concealed glee in adopting an old-fashioned and unpopular position". But surely this is a good glee, for it is the joy of the underdog, the joy in winning a battle intrinsically worth winning, the joy of telling the truth to people who do not know it and need it.

There is more than personal proclivity behind Lewis' refusal to share modernity's "chronological snobbery". There is the very practical principle that "it is not the remembered but the forgotten past that enslaves us", or, as Santayana put it, "Those who do not learn from the past are condemned to repeat it."

In light of this principle, it is indeed disastrous timing to find ignorance of the past, in the form of "chronological snobbery", arising within that particular generation of the species addicted to war which has discovered how to kill every living man on the planet; that it is this generation of the species with the death wish that has thrown away its history books and now believes itself to be the generation that will bring peace to the world.

Mention of war and killing brings us to Principle Five, which is the principle Malcolm Muggeridge has called the most unpopular of all the Christian dogmas and yet the only one empirically provable simply by reading the daily newspapers: the dogma of Original Sin.

It is this dogma which more than anything else distinguishes a conservative from a liberal. A conservative has been defined as a liberal who has just gotten mugged. In other words, conservatives believe in evil. They also believe in absolute moral standards. The two are interdependent, for if there are no moral absolutes, one man's evil is merely another man's good.

Rather than belabor the obvious with many quotations from Lewis on this point, let us only remember the whole masterly chapter in *The Problem of Pain* entitled "Human Wickedness".

A Christian is not shocked by human wickedness, by the latest scandal to hit the press. For a Christian has seen Calvary. He would not be surprised to see Lucifer fall like lightning on New York as he fell on Sodom and Gomorrah. A Christian expects to see the whole world dissolve in fervent heat, the stars fall from Heaven, and the skies roll back like a scroll; he is not unduly terrified by Hiroshima.

The God of Jesus Christ is a God of mercy and love and forgiveness, but he is also a God of justice and judgment. The very same authority that is virtually our only authority for believing that "God is love" also clearly teaches that God is just, and that those who do not meet him clothed in his gift of salvation and grace must meet him naked, without a wedding garment. For all must meet him, since he is Truth, and Truth is universal and unavoidable. Mercy is Truth clothed; judgment is Truth naked.

Five historical principles, then: skepticism about the philosophy of history; denial of historicism and its belief in the malleability of human nature; denial of Progressivism and Universal Evolutionism; denial of "chronological snobbery"; and denial of Enlightenment optimism and modern relativism and liberalism because of *their* denial of the reality of sin and judgment.

We now turn, more briefly, to four stages in Lewis' empirical description of our history: the pre-modern world, especially medieval Christendom; the Renaissance, or Great Divide between the classical and the modern; the modern world; and the future.

First, what have we lost? Describing medieval Christendom as not merely a unified social order but a unified cosmos, Lewis writes in *The Discarded Image,* "Marcus Aurelius wished that men would love the universe as a man can love his own city. I believe that something like this was really possible in the period I am discussing." For the medieval felt "like a man being conducted through an immense cathedral, not like one lost in a shoreless sea".

Yet even as his head was in the clouds, his feet were on the ground—the proper place for both. Medieval man thought of himself (to use a Chestertonian image) neither as a balloon flying loose in the sky (like our spiritualizing orientalizers and gnostics), nor as a mole burrowing in the earth (like our modern materialists), but as a tree, with roots firmly planted in the earth and branches reaching up into the heavens.

Lewis describes what a medieval boy learned in school:

> Farriery, forestry, archery, hawking, sawing, dichting, thatching, brewing, baking, weaving, and practical astronomy. This concrete knowledge mixed with their law, rhetoric, theology, and mythology had an outlook very different from our own. High abstractions and rarefied artifices jostled the earthiest particulars. . . . They talked more readily than we about large universals such as death, changes, fortune, friendship, or salvation; but also about pigs, loaves, boots and boats. The mind darted more easily to and fro between that mental heaven and earth; the cloud of middle generalizations hanging between the two was then much smaller. Hence, as it seems to us, both the naïveté and the energy of their writing. . . . They talk something like angels and something like sailors and stable boys, never like civil servants or writers of leading articles.

We moderns have lost both the solid objectivity of the high universals (especially Truth and Goodness) and of the low particulars, the concrete world. Both have been dissolved into a vague, abstract ideological-political-sociological-psychological mid-range. *We* are the "middle" ages.

The Great Divide between medieval and modern has its origins in the forces that dissipated this medieval energy: philosophical Nominalism and skepticism, clerical corruption, economic mercantilism, and biological plague. But it did not define itself until a new *summum bonum* appeared on the horizon. Bacon announces the new age with the slogans "knowledge for power" (rather than for its own sake), and "man's conquest of nature" (rather than of himself).

Of the two great spiritual revolutions in the history of Western civilization, the first from pre-Christian to Christian and the second from Christian to post-Christian, Lewis says:

> It appears to me that the second change is even more radical than the first (as divorce is more traumatic than marriage). Christians and pagans had much more in common with each other than either has with a post-Christian. The gap between those who worship different gods is not so wide as that between those who worship and those who do not. . . . [T]he gap between Professor Ryle and, say, Dante is wider than that between Dante and Virgil.

As Lewis sardonically says in the poem "A Cliché Came out of Its Cage", the world is *not* "going back to Paganism" ("Oh, bright Vision!") any more than a divorcée goes back to virginity. For technology has replaced religion at the center of our consciousness and our life. We have a new *summum bonum* — power — and a new means to it — technology, or technique.

Aristotle rated technique (technical knowledge, technē, know-how) as third on the hierarchy of values, after (1) knowledge of the truth for its own sake, and (2) practical knowledge, or knowledge for living, for acting. The modern world has simply turned this hierarchy exactly upside down, as it has turned man upside down.

Two other major changes are necessary corollaries of this change from contemplation to technique, from "conforming the soul to reality" to "conforming reality to the soul". The first is a new conception of reality. For one does not try to conform God or the gods to the wishes of the human soul, but one tries to conform nature to those wishes. Thus Naturalism replaces Supernaturalism in metaphysics. At first this means only ignoring God, then denying God, finally (worst of all), both.

The second corollary is equally crucial. It is "the poison of subjectivism", the belief that the *Tao,* moral values, are man-made. This follows from Naturalism, for if there is no God to originate values, man is the only other possible origin. But then values are only the rules of our games. If we make the rules, we can change them or break them.

Our civilization is now well advanced in its new experiment with its new God. How has it turned out? Has it made us happy or good? Has it even made us honest with ourselves? W. H. Auden answers all three questions No in his poem "September 1939":

> Faces along the bar
> Cling to their average day;
> The lights must never go out,
> The music must always play,
> Lest we know where we are:
> Lost in a haunted wood:
> Children afraid of the dark
> Who have never been happy or good.

Even Freud admits this. In his most philosophical work, *Civilization and Its Discontents,* he asks the simple but great question: If the gods were only the projections of our dreams, and if our dreams have now become true by our having become gods, "masters and possessors of nature", then why aren't we happy?

The twentieth century is the century of destruction, genocide, suicide, anxiety, and psychosis. Here is how Lewis' mouthpiece, Ransom, describes the modern world to the resuscitated Merlin in *That Hideous Strength:*

However far you went you would find the machines, the crowded cities, the empty thrones, the false writings, the barren beds: men maddened with false promises and soured with true miseries, worshipping the iron works of their own hands, cut off from Earth their mother and from the Father in Heaven. . . . The shadow of one dark wing is over all Tellus.

The Pilgrim's Regress describes our "progress" thus:

> Their labour-saving devices multiply drudgery,
> Their aphrodisiacs make them impotent,

> Their amusements bore them,
> Their rapid production of food leaves half of them
>   starving,
> And their devices for saving time have banished
>   leisure from their country.

Finally—the fourth stage of our descriptive analysis of our history according to Lewis—where are we going?

Lewis is skeptical of the philosophy of history, as we know. He claims to have no crystal ball, and is highly suspicious of all who do. But he traces a movement, a single trend, from the past into the present that can be projected into a future; a movement that is accelerating both in rapidity and intensity. The movement is, in a word, Reductionism, "that great movement of internalization [subjectivization] and that consequent aggrandisement of man and dissection of the outer universe, in which the psychological history of the West has so largely consisted" (as *The Discarded Image* puts it). As more and more things are located in our consciousness, fewer and fewer are left in objective reality. Our history is the story of King Midas: "Man with his new powers became rich like Midas, but all that he touched had gone dead and cold."

Lewis described this process in his preface to D. E. Harding's quirky, obscure, and unsuccessful attempt to reverse that process in *The Hierarchy of Heaven and Earth*:

> We can observe a single one-way progression. At the outset the universe appears packed with will, intelligence, life and positive qualities; every tree is a nymph and every planet a god. Man himself is akin to the gods. The advance of knowledge gradually empties this rich and genial universe: first of its gods, then of its colours, smells, sounds and tastes, finally of solidity itself. . . . As these items are taken from the world, they are transferred to the subjective side of the account: classified as our sensations, thoughts, images or emotions. The Subject becomes gorged, inflated at the expense of the Object.

We need now only three more principles—psychological ones this time—and we are ready to derive our prophetic conclusion.

The first is what Lewis calls the principle of "First and Second Things". Presupposing the *Tao,* the doctrine of objective values, this principle states that, whenever one of two values is really greater than another, prior to another, if man upsets this hierarchy, he loses *both* values. In other words, to sacrifice a "First Thing" to a "Second Thing" is to lose not only the "First Thing" but the "Second Thing" as well.

The principle is used extensively in *The Four Loves,* but it is first defined in 1942 in *Time and Tide,* reprinted in *God in the Dock,* about the Nazis' ideological perversions of their own Teutonic mythology. The Nazi ideologues declared that henceforth Hagen, rather than Siegfried, should be regarded as the hero of the story of the Niebelungs (since Hitler resembled the dark and crafty dwarf Hagen more than the noble and generous Siegfried). The lesson: if you subordinate high art to low politics, you pervert both. The contemporary application is that any civilization, like ours, which ranks its own mere survival above any objective values to survive for, will not survive. If you have nothing worth dying for, you will die. If you have nothing worth living for except mere living, you will not live.

> Civilizations have pursued a host of different values in the past: God's will, honour, virtues, empire, ritual, glory, mysticism, knowledge. The first and most practical question for ours is to raise the question, to care about the *summum bonum,* to have something to live for and to die for, lest we die.

He ends the prophetic essay with these prophetic words:

> There is much rash idealization of past ages about, and I do not wish to encourage more of it. Our ancestors were cruel, lecherous, greedy and stupid, like ourselves. But while they cared for other things more than for civilization . . . was civilization often in serious danger of disappearing?
>
> At least the suggestion is worth a thought. To be sure, if it

were true that civilization will never be safe till it is put second, that immediately raises the question, second to what? What is the first thing? The only reply I can offer here is that if we do not know, then the first and only truly practical thing is to set about finding out.

A second psychological principle is so common throughout Lewis' writings and shared with so many other twentieth-century writers (Orwell, Huxley, Eliot, Auden, Ortega y Gasset, David Riesman, Spengler, Ernst Becker) that I need only mention it. It is the demon of collectivism, of mob psychology, of mass consciousness. The dark side of this comfortable conformism is the death wish. Free, thinking individuals do not usually kill themselves, but lemmings, Nazis, or Jim Jones' Jonestowners do.

Our third and final psychological principle is the deepest one of all because it stems from our deepest center, our heart. It is the deepest thing in Lewis himself, according to his own admission. It is *Sehnsucht,* "Joy", the "inconsolable longing", Augustine's "restless heart".

A corollary of the "restless heart" is Aquinas' principle that "No man can live without delight. That is why a man deprived of spiritual joy goes over to carnal pleasures." "Carnal pleasures" includes violence as well as lust, and it is worth investigating at this point, in the interests of prognostications of civilizational survival, how these two things are connected.

Modern man needs somehow to assure himself of his own reality. Ever since Descartes, he has thought of himself as "the ghost in the machine", and ever since his denial of the *Tao* he has thought of himself as a free-floating spirit with no roots in eternity. To find a substitute for God as the origin of his values, he looks to the new god, "Society", i.e., the Zeitgeist, fashion. How can such a man prove he is real? How can a ghost live?

Two things no ghost can do: no ghost can murder and no ghost can rape. Entering the concrete, living reality of another human body, to kill or to copulate, to destroy or to create life forcibly, proves he is no ghost. Thus the unconscious takes its revenge; if no bright sacred mysteries anchor man's life, the dark mysteries arise. For both sex and death are great mysteries, and our unconscious still knows that even if our brains are addled by pop psychology's demythologization and trivialization of sex into a mere pleasure-function and of death into just another natural process.

Denied good sex and good death, we necessarily turn to bad sex and bad death, lust and violence, rape and war. Denied Jehovah, we turn to Moloch, for man cannot live without gods. The battles on our earth always begin in the heavens. It is Moloch come again who has devoured twenty million unborn babies with the blessing of our Supreme Court. Is it not hypocritical to ask God to deliver us from the horrors of nuclear holocaust when we "cause our sons and daughters to pass through the fire" of the great abortion holocaust? And when Moloch comes, can Lucifer be far behind?

It is time to collect our wits, our principles, and roll them into a ball to try to hit the pins of the future with them. We know in part and prophesy in part. We see our own future through a glass, darkly. Our first principle, skepticism about the philosophy of history, cautions us against anything more than a guess and a warning on the basis of our other eleven principles.

Truth is unchanging. The principles of morality are unchanging. The human essence is unchanging. Therefore there is no hope of a New Man, Heaven on Earth, Babel Rebuilt, a Brave New World, or Superman. Man has always been violent and selfish and will be until the end of time. "The poor you will always have with you", we were reminded by the most realistic of teachers. "There will be wars and rumors of wars" until the end, unless Christ was a fool or a liar; only the size of the weapons and the terror will change. Our second philosophical principle, the unchangingness of human nature, thus gives us little reason to hope.

We are *not* progressing, even within the limits of our essence and our powers, in wisdom and virtue. Modern man is not Enlightened Man but Apostate Man, and the Bible holds out little hope to apostates. Evolution may be true of the body and even of the brain, but it is not true of the soul. Our third philosophical principle, the denial of Progressivism, combined with Lewis' four-point description of our history as a slippery slope from medieval Christian fullness through Renaissance *hybris* to modern misery and nihilism—the Midas story—gives us little reason to hope. The previous point gave us little hope from our nature; this one gives us little hope from our history. Neither our unchanging essence nor our changing story looks like a progress.

Ah, but we have left behind that old pessimism, cries the modern mind. We are the people, and wisdom was born with us. Alas, replies Lewis, following Santayana, those who do not learn from history are condemned to repeat it. The refusal of this "chronological snobbery", our fourth principle, also gives us little hope.

We are still sinners, but a new kind of sinners: sinners who no longer believe in sin. That is the most dangerous kind. We are sinaholics in denial. Our fifth principle, the denial of modernity's denial of Original Sin, also sounds hopeless; for if the patient denies his disease, he will not go to the doctor. If we reject the only One who ever even claimed to save us not only from ignorance or impotence but from sin, as our civilization is increasingly doing, there is no alternative but to pay "the wages of sin", which is death.

We no longer have nuclear families or even nuclear selves, only nuclear bombs. The death within will surely spill out into a death without if we refuse the only One who can save us from both deaths.

Our first psychological principle, about "First" and "Second Things", reinforces our hopelessness, for throughout our civilization, as in our individual lives, "Second Things" are more and more replacing "First Things". We grow our toys and shrink our wisdom until the toys become enormous clubs wielded by tiny spoiled children. What happens when you give explosives to toddlers?

Our second psychological principle, the demon of collectivism, simply assures us that "we'll all go together when we go" in our global village.

And our third psychological principle, our dark and desperate search for lost joy and life and power, means we can't stop. We are addicts only pretending to be free. In reality, if we do not serve God, we must serve a demon. For we must worship something, and any idol, any nongod worshipped as God, turns into a demon. Our new god, the "conquest of nature", has turned into the demon of Lucifer's nuclear fire. Further, our collective Oedipus complex has wrought the death of God the Father and the rape of our Mother Nature. Meanwhile, our "chronological snobbery" is so strong that we do not hear or heed even the wisdom of the old margarine commercial: "It's not nice to fool Mother Nature." Nor is it safe. Nor, even, is it possible.

What, then, can we do? Are we simply doomed? Can we find any hope in Lewis, or even any advice for living in a doomed and hopeless world?

Indeed we can. Lewis would offer us at least four pieces of advice.

First, as a Christian, he would remind us of what modern Christians have forgotten for the first time in Christian history: that we are strangers and aliens in this world, spies in enemy territory. Perhaps we can do nothing to save our country, our civilization, or even our planet; but even if this is so, we must remember that "this world is not my home, I'm just a-passing through", that our true country is Heaven, and that the Church, Christ's own mystical body, is Heaven's impregnable and indestructible outpost on earth. Let us remember our only absolute *patria* and not misplace our primary patriotism. We are guaranteed survival, success, and salvation as the Church, but not as Americans, as Westerners, or as this world.

Second, we must remember what the greatest power and the greatest task and the greatest success is. There is more power in one atom of Christ's body than in all the atom bombs in the universe. There is a greater glory in saving our sanity and our souls than in saving our civilization. And there is a greater success in contributing one tiny link in a long chain which God will use to pull a single soul out of the pit of modern error than in single-handedly perfecting and perpetuating the pit, in inventing success, satisfaction, security, and survival for our civilization. It is a greater thing to invent a single word or a single deed of charity which would sway one soul to turn to God than to invent a planet-wide system of successful Star Wars defense hardware.

In the third place, Lewis is no doomsday determinist, for divine grace, forgiveness, and hope of salvation are always held out to our choice, as a civilization as well as individuals. All the prophets say this. They appeal to free choice. They blame men for having made the wrong choice (thus assuming it was made freely, for one does not blame machines) and exhort them to change to the right choice, to turn, to repent (again assuming the freedom to do so). Lewis does the same. Here is his most prophetic passage of all about modern civilization, from *Miracles:*

> All over the world, until quite modern times, the direct insight of the mystics and the reasonings of the philosophers percolated to the mass of the people by authority and tradition; they could be received by those who were no great reasoners themselves in the concrete form of myth and ritual and the whole pattern of life. In the conditions produced by a century or so of Naturalism, plain men are being forced to bear burdens which plain men were never expected to bear before. We must get the truth ourselves or go without it. There may be two explanations for this. It might be that humanity, in rebelling against tradition and authority, has made a ghastly mistake.... On the other hand, it may be that the Power which rules our species is at this moment carrying out a daring experiment. Could it be intended

that the whole mass of the people should now move forward and occupy for themselves those heights which were once reserved only for the sages? Is the distinction between wise and simple to disappear because all are now expected to become wise? If so, our present blunderings would be but growing pains.

How hopeful! But also how sternly serious and demanding:

> But let us make no mistake about our necessities. If we are content to go back and become humble plain men obeying a tradition, well. If we are ready to climb and struggle on till we become sages ourselves, better still. But the man who will neither obey wisdom in others nor adventure for her himself is fatal.

Finally, how can we work toward this hope for our civilization? What can we *do* for the peace and survival that comes only through wisdom?

It is good to work for peace in whatever social and political ways really do work, whether this means working for disarmament or for stronger armaments. We do not know with certainty which way will work best on the political level (though we nearly always claim we do). But we *do* know with certainty (because God himself has told us) what will work on the spiritual level, and we also know that that level cuts deeper and works at the roots. So to anyone who is concerned with peace and with the life and survival of our civilization, here is a summary in a single paragraph of what I have learned from my master C. S. Lewis:

Sodom and Gomorrah almost made it. If God had found but ten righteous men, he would have spared two whole cities. Abraham's intercession nearly saved Sodom, and it did save Lot. We must be Abrahams. Charles Williams said that "the altar must often be built in one place so that the fire from Heaven may come down at another." It is also true that the altar must be built and prayer and sacrifice made at one place so that the fire from Hell may not come down at another. It can be done. The most important thing each of us can do to save the world from holocaust and from Hell, from nuclear destruction and from spiritual destruction, is the most well-known, most unoriginal thing in the world: to love God with our whole heart and soul and mind and strength and to love our neighbors as ourselves.

You the individual can make a difference. You can be the straw that breaks the camel's back, the vote that wins the election. You can save the world.

2

Darkness at Noon: The Eclipse of "The Permanent Things"

We all know what Christianity looks like when viewed from the standpoint of modernity. In this chapter I shall try to turn the truth tables and see what modernity looks like when viewed from the standpoint of Christianity.

My point of view is what C. S. Lewis called "mere Christianity". "Mere Christianity" means not "little Christianity" but "big Christianity": full, biblical, apostolic, traditional, orthodox Christianity.

I shall be using many of Lewis' ideas in this chapter, some explicitly, some implicitly. But this is not a scholarly essay about Lewis but an amateur essay using Lewis (and others) to think about the fate of "the permanent things" in the modern world. (I'm sure Lewis would much prefer his readers to think *with* him rather than *about* him; to look *along* with him rather than *at* him—to use his own very useful distinction from the essay "Meditation in a Toolshed".)

We know what Christianity looks like when viewed from the standpoint of modernity because we are bombarded with this. The media moguls, the opinion molders and real educators of our

This chapter originally appeared in *Faith and Reason,* vol. 17, no. 1 (Spring 1991), Christendom Press, Front Royal, Virginia.

society, are the most aggressively anti-Christian propaganda elite since the Nazis. Can you remember a single movie in the last twenty years in which some or all of the Christian clergymen were not hypocrites?

But what does modernity look like from the viewpoint of Christianity? Essentially, a gallows on which "the permanent things" are lynched without a trial; an altar on which "the permanent things" are sacrificed to the dark gods of Baal and Ashtaroth and Moloch: power and greed and lust.

Our world was aptly described by Arthur Koesteler in a book with the paradoxical and prophetic title *Darkness at Noon.* A similar title by Martin Buber, *Eclipse of God,* makes the same point by a similar astronomical image. We are now living in the real Dark Ages, as we approach the end of that century which a famous religious journal named itself after with incredible naïveté and false prophecy, "The Christian Century"! If there is any title we can be certain the history books of the future will *never* use for our century, it is that one. Much more likely is Franky Schaeffer's suggestion, "The Century of Genocide".

Of all twentieth-century inventions, the latter one is the one that has most drastically affected the most lives. We have so far witnessed five major holocausts in this century, and along with every "civilized" nation in the Western world except Ireland, Portugal, and Malta, we are now participating in the sixth and largest one of all, the only one that shows no signs of ending as the other five did. What the Turks did to the Armenians, Hitler to the Jews, Stalin and Mao to their political enemies, and Pol Pot to one-third of his nation's people, our present femininity-haters (the incredibly misnamed "radical feminists") and their allies are still doing to the tiniest, most innocent, and most defenseless of all classes of human beings, unborn babies.

Mother Teresa said, with the simplicity of a peasant, "When a mother can kill her own child, what is left of the West to save?" (Incredibly, *Time* magazine printed that statement. Perhaps there is some hope after all.)

God asked a rhetorical question in Scripture: "Can a mother forsake the fruit of her womb? Even if she could, I could not forsake you, says the Lord your God." The rhetorical question was meant to put forth an unthinkable absurdity. Yet millions of mothers today perform that unthinkable absurdity, and many more millions, mostly men, think approvingly of that unthinkable work of Moloch.

Doubtless, most of the twenty million mothers who have aborted their babies since our Supreme Court declared this injustice were themselves victims of propaganda pressures and cultural conditioning, "more sinned against than sinning". That, however, makes things worse, not better: it implicates the whole culture in the double deed of destroying undeveloped bodies and undeveloped consciences.

If the soul is more precious than the body, the latter death is worse than the former. The soul of Western civilization is dying; that is the essence of our tragedy. When its body follows, as it must, we will see the civilizational pus ooze, but that pus is already there, festering inside. The barbarians are already within the gates. They write the textbooks, newspapers, TV shows, movies, and music.

Is this going to be another one of those tedious sermons on how to prevent the wreck of Western civilization? No. For as Whittaker Chambers wrote, "It is idle to talk about preventing the wreck of Western civilization. It is already a wreck from within."

Do I come to you then as a prophet of doom? No. I disavow both mantles, both prophet and doom. Perhaps there is still time to intercede for the secular city as Abraham interceded for Sodom. We do not know how much time we have left. But we do know this: if God spares New York, he will owe an apology to Sodom.

Avery Dulles has mapped out, in a kind of logical square of opposition, a useful chart of four possible contemporary Christian attitudes toward our secular society. He calls the four options traditionalism, neo-conservatism, liberalism, and radicalism. Traditionalism believes in the Church but not the State, i.e., not the present state of society. It is counter-cultural. Neo-conservatism believes in both the Church and the American state. Liberalism believes in Americanism but not in the Church, i.e., not traditional Christianity. And radicalism says, "A plague on both your houses."

I am a traditionalist, as was C. S. Lewis. But I want to interject a word of caution to my fellow traditionalists. It is the fear that traditionalists run the same kind of risk in idealizing the past as both neo-conservatives and liberals (what strange bedfellows!) run in looking benignly at the present and the future. Looking back is a posture that has been known to be very dangerous to one's health, especially if one is on a salt-free diet: remember Lot's wife.

So let us look to the future. Is it not time to be optimistic now that the Iron Curtain has fallen with an iron thud? To answer this question, let us ask two other questions, one about us and one about "them".

The one about us is: Were we more moved by the fear of God or the fear of Gorbachev? Were we wrestling against principalities and powers in the Kremlin or in Hell? Do we understand Solzhenitsyn's line about the border between good and evil running not between nations but down the middle of our own souls?

And the question about "them" is: What kind of freedom was uppermost in the minds of most of the masses who poured through the newly opened Berlin Wall? Was it spiritual freedom, or even intellectual freedom? Did they, like the wise men from the East of old, come West seeking Christ? Or condoms? Did they pour into churches? Or porno shops? What excited them about the West? Did they buy Bibles or toilet paper? What freedom was legislated in Romania as soon as it had killed its dictator, who was guilty of enormous crimes? It was the freedom to kill those who are guilty of no crime at all except being in the way of someone who was bigger and already born.

So let us look to the real battle, not to the fake one. Now that that silly little temporary distraction called Communism is dead or dying everywhere from Managua to Moscow—everywhere except Cambridge and Columbia—we can get back to the battle that should have been bothering traditionalists all along much more than the battle against the Eastern barbarianism without, namely, the Western barbarianism within. The year 1984 has come and gone with few signs of Orwell's *1984* looming on our horizon, but Huxley's *Brave New World* looks like a more accurate prophecy every year. So let us be brave and look at our new world, at the internal slippery slope we've been sliding down, now that the external pseudo-threat of Communism has lost its power to distract our attention.

We're all familiar with the statistics on violent crime, rape, child abuse, drugs, and similar American leisure activities. We know that half of all marriages commit suicide, i.e., divorce. We can read headlines well enough to be largely cynical about financiers and politicians. Surveys tell us this is the first generation in American history whose children are less well educated than their parents. They tell us that if teenagers don't have sex, they must be ugly, isolated, or Fundamentalists. Half of all urban teenagers get pregnant, and half of them have abortions. One out of every three babies conceived is killed. A brave new world indeed.

I don't think we need to specify any more of the many symptoms of our decay. They are ubiquitous, obvious, and odious. The very word "decay" is evidence for our decay; for, as Chesterton put it, "Our fathers said that a nation had sinned and suffered, like a man; we say it has decayed, like a cheese."

Consider just one more linguistic symptom of our decay. Whenever you hear a liberal theologian calling for a more "adult" Christianity, please remember what the word "adult" means in our culture. (What is an "adult" bookstore, or an "adult" movie?) Ask yourself then what is the relationship between such a theologian and a certain old, out-of-date teacher who said, "Unless you become as little children, you cannot enter the Kingdom of God."

What happened? An eclipse. Nietzsche called it "the death of God", but Buber replied with the alternative image of the "eclipse of God". When the sun is eclipsed, it is still there but no longer seen. When someone is dead, he's no longer *there*. But both death and eclipse produce a similar effect in our experience: darkness.

It is a "darkness at noon", as Koesteler's title says, because noon is when eclipses happen. This is true both astronomically and historically. The noonday devil of pride arranges for the eclipse. It's the old Greek *hybris* plot, and it's been repeated many times: ancient Israel, Greece, Rome, America. Today secularism, sub-jectivism, relativism, materialism, and hedonism are the craters on the moon that has risen up to eclipse the sun of God just at the noon hour of human pride and cleverness, the triumph of "man's conquest of Nature". Just as Lewis prophetically warned in *The Abolition of Man,* the culmination of "man's conquest of Nature" has been his conquest of *human* nature by "liberating" it from the constraints of the natural moral law, the *Tao.*

The change is not merely that we are behaving like beasts, but that we are believing like beasts. Man has never obeyed the *Tao* very well, but he at least believed in it, and thus felt guilt. The new philosophy has removed guilt. It has made hypocrisy impos-sible, for "hypocrisy is the tribute vice pays to virtue."

Nietzsche's "death of God" is a real event, but wrongly described. It is not the death of God but of his image in the human soul. It is not the sun that is in darkness during an eclipse, as it seems, but the earth. "The death of God" is a psychological projection by a spiritual corpse.

Now when the symptoms of a terminal disease appear, whether in an individual or in a civilization, what is the reasonable thing to do? Not to despair but to treat them. Not keeping our nose to the symptoms and frothing at the mouth. Rather, we must approach the problem coldly, calmly, and logically, as a doctor would. We must be both practical and scientific. To be practical is to find out what to do and then do it. To be scientific is to ask for a clear, step-by-step analysis of the problem and its solution.

Such an analysis should use the most practical and pervasive idea in all scientific thinking, the principle of causality. Every medical analysis follows the principle of causality by going through four steps: observation, diagnosis, prognosis, and prescription. (1) Observe the symptoms; (2) diagnose the disease that causes the symptoms; (3) form a prognosis of the cure; and (4) prescribe the treatment that causes the cure. The symptoms are the bad effects, the diagnosis tells the bad cause, the prognosis the good effect, and the prescription the good cause.

Every practical philosophy answers these four questions because a practical philosopher is a doctor for the soul. For instance, Buddha's "Four Noble Truths" follow exactly these four steps. The "Four Noble Truths" comprise the whole of Buddhism, according to Buddha himself in the "Arrow Sermon": (1) to live is to suffer; all life is suffering; (2) the cause of suffering is selfish desire; (3) there is a way to end suffering and achieve Nirvana; namely, to end desire (take away the cause and you take away its effect); (4) the way to end desire is to practice the "Noble Eightfold Path", the Buddhist yoga of ego-reduction.

Freudianism also contains these four steps. (1) The symptoms are neurosis and psychosis; (2) the diagnosis says the cause is the conflict between id and superego, between individual animal desire and social norms; (3) the prognosis is homeostasis, or adjustment, a compromise of sorts; and (4) the prescription is psychoanalysis.

Marxism sees (1) the symptoms as class conflict, (2) the diagnosis as Capitalism, (3) the prognosis as the classless Communist society, and (4) the prescription as a worldwide proletarian revolution.

Platonism sees (1) the symptoms as vice; (2) the diagnosis as ignorance; (3) the prognosis as virtue; and (4) the prescription as philosophical wisdom via the Socratic method.

Christianity also fits this pattern. The symptom is death, the diagnosis is sin, the prognosis is salvation, and the prescription is repentance and faith in Christ. "The wages of sin is death, but the gift of God is eternal life in Christ Jesus our Lord" (Rom 6:23). That single sentence sums up all Christian theology.

Let us now apply the generic form of this four-step analysis to the particular content of the deadly disease in contemporary Western civilization.

The first of the four steps in the analysis is the observation of the symptoms. I think we all pretty much know both that the patient is critical and what the symptoms are, so I shall skip step one and spend most of my time on step two, the diagnosis.

For that is what we mainly go to the doctor for. We go to the doctor only after we have already observed the symptoms, otherwise we wouldn't be there. "Those who are sick need a physician, not those who are well. I come to call not the righteous, but sinners" (Mt 9:12).

And once the doctor performs step two, once he diagnoses the disease, steps three and four usually follow fairly routinely. Once you know the disease, you can consult the textbooks to see whether it can be cured (the prognosis) and, if so, how (the prescription).

I am going to diagnose our disease as an "eclipse of 'the permanent things'". Therefore we need some definitions. I already defined "eclipse", but not "permanent" or "things". What "things" are permanent? And in what way are they "permanent"?

We can mean three different things by "permanent" and three different things by "things". First, "permanent". How can anything be permanent? Essentially, either objectively or subjectively, or both, or neither.

First, something may be permanent both objectively, in itself, and also subjectively, in our consciousness, e.g., the Law of Causality: nothing ever arises without a cause, *and* everyone knows that. Both the fact and the knowledge of it are permanent.

Second, something may be permanent objectively but not

subjectively—for instance, the truth of monotheism. If there is one God, he is permanent and eternal, but the world's knowledge of him is not.

Third, something may be permanent subjectively but not objectively: a permanent *illusion,* such as the attractiveness of sin, or the egocentric perspective which we carry around with us all the time, as if I had first dibs on the name "I AM" rather than God.

Fourth, something may be permanent neither objectively nor subjectively, such as fads and fashions. These do not concern us here because they are not in any sense "permanent things". The other three are.

Take the crucial example of the *Tao,* moral values, the natural moral law. There are four possible positions about it. First, that it is permanent both objectively and subjectively, that there are eternal moral verities and that our awareness of them can never be eradicated from the human heart. This is the position of Saint Thomas Aquinas.

Second, that the moral law is permanent objectively but not subjectively; that we can be changed into what Lewis in *The Abolition of Man* calls "men without chests", men whose chest, or heart, or conscience, or organ for apprehending the *Tao,* has atrophied. (For a comparison between Aquinas and Lewis on this point, see Chapter 4.)

Third, that the moral law is *not* objectively permanent but that it *is* subjectively permanent, a structural illusion of the psyche. This is Freud's position: the superego is the unconscious reflection of society's constraints on the id's desires.

Fourth, that there is no objectively permanent moral law *and* no subjectively permanent moral law; that human nature is malleable and that conscience can be shaped, reshaped, or eradicated by social engineering. This is the position of Marx and of Behaviorism.

I make no apologies for calling Freud a fraud or for giving low marks to Marx, but I feel fear and trembling in arguing against

Aquinas. Yet my daily experience of ordinary American life seems to tell me that the heart, the moral organ, has indeed atrophied. Perhaps the blood needed by the heart has migrated south to another, less subtle organ. There seems to be linguistic evidence for that, for the same people who confuse "adult" and "adulterous" also often confuse "organism" and "orgasm".

Well, I don't want to spend my time in this chapter arguing whether the moral law is subjectively permanent or not, but I want to ask instead what things are objectively permanent. What kinds of "things" are "the permanent things", anyway? Certainly not concrete things, like concrete. What, then? Three things, at least.

First, permanent *truths.* These are not simply *ideas* in human minds, because our minds are *not* permanent. We change our minds faster than we change our clothes. If these "permanent things" are ideas, they must be in the divine mind.

These permanent truths are not even the so-called "laws of nature", or laws of science. Heraclitus, the pre-Socratic Greek philosopher, first clearly realized the double truth that all matter is in motion and that there are permanent laws or formulas for this motion. He taught that "everything flows", like a river, but also that there was a permanent *logos* or law of change. For him, this was the law of the transformations between fire and water, earth and air; for us, it is such truths as the law of transformation between mass and energy ($E = MC^2$) or the equality between force and mass times acceleration.

But these laws of nature are not what I mean by "the permanent things". For they are only descriptions of how matter does behave, not laws of how it must behave. Molecules do not bow down before a pre-existing "Ten Commandments of Matter" before they set out on their daily rounds. There is no permanent necessity to the laws of nature. It is conceivable that they may change billions of years from now if and when all the matter in the universe gets sucked into Black Holes. It is generally agreed today that the laws of nature were radically different during the first few seconds of the universe's existence, right after the Big Bang from what they are now.

No, by permanent truths I mean things like the Law of Non-Contradiction, and the Law of Causality, and the multiplication table: the objective and unchangeable laws of logic, metaphysics, and mathematics. Nothing can ever both be and not be in the same way at the same time. Nothing can ever begin to be without any cause at all for its beginning to be. Two times three can never begin to equal seven.

Can anyone deny these "permanent things"? Yes indeed. Even *they* are not subjectively permanent. For many of our currently fashionable philosophies reduce them to symbol systems, useful conventions, mental biases, cultural copings, projections of our fear of death or chaos, word games, or even patriarchal plots to oppress women. Permanent objective truths are not necessarily permanent subjectively. I spent eighteen dollars for a badly written book by Allan Bloom because I got hooked on its wonderful first sentence: "If there is one thing every college professor in America can be certain of, or nearly certain of, it is that all or nearly all of the students who enter his classroom will believe, or think they believe, that truth is relative."

Why would someone want to deny objective truth? Who's afraid of the Law of Non-Contradiction? What's behind the insane attempt to soften up the very structures of sanity? I think it is not logical, mathematical, or metaphysical truths that threaten them, but *moral* truths. If there were permanent moral truths, that would mean that morality is no longer about nice, warm, fuzzy, vague, soft, negotiable things called "values" but about hard, unyielding, uncompromising, uncomfortable, nonnegotiable things called "laws".

And their fear of permanent, objective moral laws is amazingly selective. It almost always comes down to just one area: sex.

In my experience, students, like professors, bluff a lot and do adroit intellectual dancing. But I'd bet a wad of money that if only the sixth commandment were made optional, nearly all the hatred and fear of the Church would vanish.

Saint Augustine was one of the few honest enough to admit his obsession. After puffing great philosophical profundities about the intellectual problems that kept him back from the Church, he finally admits in the *Confessions,* "The plain fact was, I thought I should be impossibly miserable without the embraces of a mistress." If *that* profoundly philosophical motive was what held back one of the most honest, truth-seeking wisdom-lovers in history, do you really hope that nobler ideals motivate the spiritual children of Woodstock?

Thus, much more crucial than permanent *truths* are permanent *values,* or rather, permanent *moral laws,* laws as objective and unchangeable as the laws of mathematics. *Applying* these laws may be uncertain and changeable, but *they* are not. Applying the laws of mathematics is also sometimes uncertain and changeable, e.g., when you try to measure the exact length of a live alligator.

(By the way, I think Lewis made a tactical error in conceding to use the modern word "values" instead of the ancient word "law" in *The Abolition of Man.* For to the mind of the modern reader, the idea of "objective values" is simply an unintelligible contradiction in terms. For this modern mind is Cartesian and Kantian; and to the Cartesian dualist, "objective" means merely "physical", which values are *not,* and to the Kantian moralist, "values" mean something posited by man's will, not God's: something subjective, though universal. You see, there is real confusion here. God did not give Moses "The Ten Values". And the currently fashionable way of teaching moral relativism in American high schools is not called "Laws Clarification". There *is* a difference.)

A third kind of "permanent things" emphasizes the word "things". Not only are there permanent *truths* and permanent *moral laws,* but also permanent *things.* There is a wonderful passage about this in *Till We Have Faces.* After Orual's sister Psyche tells Orual that she has seen the face of the god, her husband, and his palace, Orual wonders whether it could be true even though she cannot see these things. She asks her Greek tutor and philosopher, the Fox:

> "You don't think—not possibly—not as a mere hundredth chance—there might be things that are real though we can't see them?"
>
> "Certainly I do. Such things as Justice, Equality, the Soul, or musical notes."
>
> "Oh, Grandfather, I don't mean things like that.... Are there no things—I mean *things*—but what we see?"[1]

The "things" Orual suspects are not physical things, yet they are not abstract ideas, either. They are solid and substantial and real, like gods or Platonic Forms. The immense difficulty modern students have in understanding Plato's famous theory of Forms as anything other than abstract class concepts can be seen from their utter incomprehension (yet fascination) with Charles Williams' novel *The Place of the Lion,* in which the very real and active protagonists are Platonic Forms (!).

These Platonic universals are not abstractions. They are *things.* They are gods, or spirits. In "The Descent of the Gods" chapter of *That Hideous Strength,* each of the planetary spirits is both a universal quality, like joviality, and a particular entity, like Jove. Jove, or Jupiter, does not merely *symbolize* joy; he *is* joy. Joy is not an abstract property, but a "permanent *thing*", a reality, a god.

Lewis is so insistent on this point about the concreteness, not abstractness, of nonphysical realities that in *Miracles* he goes so far as to call God himself a particular thing. He says:

> What we know through laws and general principles is a series of connections. But in order for there to be a real universe, the connections must be given something to connect: a torrent of opaque actualities must be fed into the pattern. If God created

[1] C. S. Lewis, *Till We Have Faces* (St. James Place, London: Collins, Son & Co., 1979), 150.

the world, then He is precisely the source of this torrent. . . . But if God is the ultimate source of all concrete, individual things and events, then God Himself must be concrete and individual in the highest degree. Unless the origin of all other things were itself concrete and individual, nothing else could be so; for there is no conceivable means whereby what is abstract or general could itself produce concrete reality. Bookkeeping continued to all eternity could never produce one farthing. Metre, of itself, could never produce a poem.

. . . if by using the word 'infinite' we encourage ourselves to think of God as a formless 'everything' about whom nothing in particular and everything in general is true, then it would be better to drop the word altogether. Let us dare to say that God is a particular Thing. Once, He was the only Thing; but He created, He made other things to be. He is not those other things. He is not 'universal being'. . . . He has a determinate character. Thus He is righteous, not amoral; creative, not inert. . . . And men are exhorted to 'know the Lord,' to discover and experience this particular character.[2]

We have defined three kinds of "permanent things". All three are in eclipse in our civilization. Now I want to concentrate especially on the second one, the moral "things", and on *The Abolition of Man.*

One of the things this book does for our culture is to show us ourselves in our radical distinctiveness from all previous cultures. The most radically new feature of our civilization is not technology, its newly powerful means, but the lack of a *summum bonum,* an end. We are the first civilization that does not know why we exist.

Every past civilization has had some religious answer to that question. The essence of modernity is the abandoning of that religious foundation, and thus eventually also abandoning the moral first story of the same civilizational building. Morality has always rested on religion in practice, even if a few philosophers like Plato and Aristotle could defend it without religion in theory.

---

[2] C. S. Lewis, *Miracles* (New York: Macmillan), 86, 88.

Dostoyevsky wrote, "If God does not exist, everything is permissible." History shows far more people, both atheists and theists, on Dostoyevsky's side than on Plato's here. For Sartre, "there can be no eternal truth since there is no infinite and perfect consciousness to think it." For Nietzsche, the consequence of the new gospel that "God is dead" is a "transvaluation of all values". Like Milton's Satan, he says, in effect, "Evil, be thou my good." He declares love, compassion, mercy, justice, impartiality, and democracy to be weak and therefore evil; cruelty, ruthlessness, war, competition, and selfishness are good. For from the natural struggle of selfishnesses emerges the strongest, the Superman.

Please do not be horrified, but I am often tempted to thank God for Hitler. For if one big Hitler and one big Holocaust had not scared the Hell out of us, we might be living in a worldwide Hitler-Holocaust-Hell right now. God rubbed our face in it—we have seen the pure logical consequences of "the death of God" in the fires of Auschwitz. Yet most of us in the West still have not learned the old and simple lesson (scandalous to modern intellectuals simply because it is simple and old) that "unless the Lord build the house, they labor in vain who build it." No one in our time has ever faced and answered the question: If there is no God, *why shouldn't I* do as I please if I can get away with it? Because it's not "acceptable", nice, humane, human, democratic, fair, just, community-building, helpful, survival-enhancing, practical, and approved? But suppose I don't *want* to be "acceptable", nice, humane, human, democratic, fair, just, community-building, helpful, survival-enhancing, practical, or approved? I have never heard any reply to that from any humanist. No one has ever answered Dostoyevsky's "Underground Man". The existentialists refute humanism. You don't need an Augustine or an Aquinas to refute humanism, only a Nietzsche or a Sartre.

For there is no morality without real moral laws, binding duties, objective obligations. A morality of mere convention, man-made and thus man-revisable rules of the social game, is not morality at all, only *mores.* Life under such pseudomorality is not real moral warfare, only war *games,* and we are never on the hot seat, but in a hot tub.

So there is no morality without moral absolutes. But there can be no moral absolutes without God. That's the second step. An absolute law can come from and be enforced only by an absolute will. Finally, no civilization can stand without morality. That should be exceedingly obvious, both from common sense and from history. Thus, without religion, no moral absolutes; without moral absolutes, no real morality; and without real morality, no survival of civilization. Thus without religion, civilization cannot survive.

And it has not survived. This is not just a law of logic but also a law of history. Every civilization in history has had a religious base. Ours is experimenting with a deviation from history's most obvious and universal law. Thus the prognosis does not look very hopeful.

This fact comes as a surprise only to this generation, the first to be biblically illiterate. All I have done is to translate into abstract, philosophical language the simple, punchy point of Old Testament history that a nation's *fate* rests on its *faith.*

There is one thing even stupider than modernism abandoning religion in society: theological modernism abandoning religion even in religion. The essence of theological modernism is the denial of the supernatural (miracles, Christ's divinity and Resurrection, Heaven and Hell, the Second Coming, and the divine inspiration of Scripture). Modernism reduces religion to morality, morality to social morality, and social morality to Socialism.

In fact, its instinctive gravitation to Socialism is natural. For Socialism and religion are the only two answers to a problem Lewis poses in *The Abolition of Man:* the problem of the Controllers versus the controlled, the Conditioners versus the conditioned. To see this, we must first review his argument in that book.

Lewis' argument in chapter 3 is absolutely stunning, both in the sense of intellectually *brilliant* and in the sense of emotionally *terrifying.* It is that "man's conquest of Nature" without the *Tao* must necessarily become Nature's conquest of man. For "man's conquest of Nature" must always mean, in the concrete, some men's power over other men, using nature as the instrument. Lewis' examples of the wireless, the airplane, and the contraceptive show this: some men wield the newly won power over others as its patients. Perhaps they are its willing patients, but they are its patients. Now as long as both the agents and the patients of these powers over nature admit and work within a common *Tao,* they have the same interests, rights, and values. Monarchy is not oppressive if the king and the people are working for a common goal under a common law and share a common dignity. But if the power elite, whether king, voting majority, or media elite, cease to believe in an objective *Tao,* as is clearly the case in our society, then they become Controllers, Conditioners, and social engineers, and the patients become the controlled. Propaganda replaces propagation. Propagation is "old birds teaching young birds to fly". Propaganda is programming parrots. Propagation is the transmission of tradition. Propaganda is the invention of innovation. Which of the two is piped into our brains daily by our media?

This new class of Innovators, the *Tao*-less Conditioners, will themselves be motivated in their social engineering, but not by the *Tao,* which is supernatural and eternal, a "permanent thing". Instead, they will be motivated by their natural impulses, which are nonpermanent things: their heredity and environment, especially their environment, especially fashionable opinions. This means they will be motivated by Nature, not by "the permanent things", which are supernatural.

Thus "man's conquest of Nature" must be expanded at both ends: the conquerors are themselves conquered by Nature (*Tao*-less environment), and they in turn only use nature to conquer other men. This is why "man's conquest of Nature" turns out to be Nature's conquest of man. Man's triumph is thus man's abolition, for the new man is an artifact. Those who have been conditioned out of the belief in free will lose their free will. Those who believe they are only clever apes become only clever apes. "Made in U.S.A." comes to mean "made in the image of King Kong", not King Christ. Where is Christ? In a jar of Andres Serrano's urine.

Now there are only two ways out of this "abolition of man" by social engineering. One is, of course, the return to the *Tao*. This is unlikely because the one thing modernity resists the most is return. It believes in progress, not repentance. But this would be a solution to the alienation between the Conditioners and the conditioned because both would then be under the same moral law. That spiritual equality would overshadow the physical and social inequality. The authorities would then wield power only in the name of the common objective *Tao*.

The other way to unity is socialism: not spiritual unity of a *Tao* but mere physical unity, i.e., social unity, i.e., economic unity. A "classless society" will supposedly make it impossible for one class to conquer or condition others. From the history of secular socialist and communist experiments that we have seen so far, I think we must not only call all the experiments failures but also call most of the experimenters liars and hypocrites. The most systematic oppression and mass murders in history have been carried out in the name of social equality and blessed by the intellectuals.

Socialism's dream is naïve because mere equality does not automatically destroy oppression. Egalitarianism can be as oppressive as any tyranny. De Tocqueville pointed out long ago that democratic totalitarianism is not a contradiction in terms and that Americans are naïve if they think that the sheer political structure of democracy will protect them against totalitarianism. For democracy and totalitarianism are not opposite answers to the same question, but answers to two different questions, and thus can be compatible. Democracy is an answer to the question: *In whom* is the social-political power located? Its answer is: in the people at large. Totalitarianism is an answer to the question: How *much* power are the social-political authorities to have? Its answer is:

total power, power to reshape human life, human thought, human nature itself.

Here are three examples of Democratic Totalitarianism: in theory, Rousseau's "General Will" (*vox populi, vox dei*); in fiction, Huxley's *Brave New World;* and in fact, the American media establishment.

Only the *Tao* can ensure freedom. Only when we are bound to a higher law of permanent, unchangeable, objective moral absolutes are we free from being determined by the lower laws of animal instincts, selfishness, sin, and propaganda. Only conformity to the trans-social *Tao* can make nonconformity to a decadent society just, or even possible. For we do, and must, conform to something, or else we are formless. The only question is: To what? There are only two possible answers: to what is higher than ourselves or to what is lower, supernature or nature, the Bible or MTV, Jesus Christ or Ted Turner, the Crucified or the crucifiers.

Let's take a time-out and take stock for a moment. How far down the slide have we slid? How much of the *Tao* is already lost? How many of the objectively permanent things have become subjectively impermanent?

I count at least thirty-three: silence, solitude, detachment, self-control, contemplation, awe, humility, hierarchy, modesty, chastity, reverence, authority, obedience, tradition, honor, simplicity, loyalty, gentlemanliness, manliness, womanliness, propriety, ceremony, cosmic justice, pure passion, holy poverty, respect for old age, the positive spiritual use of suffering, gratitude, fidelity, real individuality, real community, courage, and absolute honesty (the passionate, or fanatical, love of truth for its own sake). That's one lost value for each of the years in Christ's life.

We could, of course, profitably spend hours, days, perhaps lifetimes exploring each one of these thirty-three lost values; and we could probably add thirty-three more. But in this age of progress and time-saving devices we have no time for such important things any more—things like conversation, debate, meditation, prayer, deep friendship, imagination, even family. (If the sexual revolution doesn't do the family in, it will die for lack of time.)

But you may think this gloomy picture I have painted of a spiritual Dark Ages is only half the picture. What of all the progress we've made?

Well, let's look at the progress we've made. It can be divided into two kinds: spiritual and material. Let's take spiritual progress first. I think there *has* been some significant spiritual progress in modernity in at least one area: kindness versus cruelty. I think we are much kinder than our ancestors were, especially to those we used to be cruel to: criminals, heretics, foreigners, other races, and especially the handicapped. I think this is very real progress indeed. I wonder, though, whether one big step forward offsets thirty-three steps back, some of them also big, some medium-sized, but none small.

In any case, the case for progress and modernity usually rests either on one of two grounds: either supposed spiritual progress that is not progress at all (e.g., freedom from superstition, authority, absolutist morality, biblical literalism, Church dogma, and the like), or explicitly material progress (e.g., scientific and technological progress). It is this last area which is spectacular and indisputable and thus the strongest case for Progressivism.

Our civilization certainly has produced astounding, magnificent, utterly undreamed-of successes in understanding and mastering the forces of nature. I think every intelligent man born before the Renaissance, if transported by a time machine to today, would be stupefied with wonder, marvel, and admiration at the awesome progress in science and technology, i.e., material progress, in our world.

But now I ask a strange, unusual, and very upsetting question: Is there such a thing as material progress at all? Or is this a confusion of categories, like a blue number, or a rectangular value? I am not sure of this, but I want to suggest, for your consideration, the possibility that there is not and cannot be any such thing as purely material progress; that only spirit can progress.

The reason I think this surprising and unpopular conclusion is true has something to do with the nature of time. To see this, we must speak Greek for a minute. The Greek language is much richer and subtler than English when it comes to philosophical distinctions, and Greek has two words for time, not just one. *Kronos* means the time measured objectively, impersonally, and mathematically by the motion of unconscious matter through space. For instance, one day of *kronos* is always exactly twenty-four hours long, the time it takes for the earth to rotate. *Kairos,* on the other hand, is human time, lived time, experienced time, the time measured by human consciousness and purposive reaching-out into a future that is not yet but is planned for. Only *kairos* knows anything of goals and values.

For instance, when Saint Paul writes, "It is now time to rise from sleep, because your salvation is nearer than when you first believed", he does not mean by "time" something like "June 30 of the year 50 A.D." "It is now time to die" does not mean "it is 3:20 P.M." Ends, goals, and purposes measure *kairos,* and these things exist only in consciousness and in spirit, not in mere matter.

The reason why I think only spirit can progress is because only spirit lives in *kairos.* For only *kairos* touches eternity, knows eternity, aims at eternity. Progress means not merely change, but change toward a goal. The change is relative and shifting, but the goal is absolute and permanent. If not, if the goal changed along with the movement toward it, we could not speak any more of progress, only change. There is no progress if the goal line recedes in front of the runner as fast as the runner runs. You can't steal second base if the second baseman has already stolen it and is running to third.

Think of a circle, like a pie, with a segment, like a piece of pie, in it. The segment is *kairos,* lived time, lifetime. The circumference is *kronos. Kronos* limits how much *kairos* there is (e.g., eighty years), but it does not determine the other dimension of *kairos,* the dimension of progress. Progress means getting closer to the goal, which in my geometrical image is symbolized by the center of the circle. That would be eternity, permanence. Only in the *kairos* dimension, i.e., the spiritual dimension, can we speak meaningfully of progress at all. The only thing *kronos* can do is endlessly circle around the center and limit the quantity of any segment of *kairos*, but the circumference is equidistant from the center. This symbolizes the fact that our lived time, our lifetime, can move toward eternity, but purely material time cannot. You get closer to God by sanctity, not by aging. The world gets closer to God by improving spiritually, not by improving materially. And God is the goal, the measure of progress.

The essence of modernity is the death of the spiritual. A modernist is someone who is more concerned about air pollution than soul pollution. A modernist is someone who wants clean air so he can breathe dirty words.

A modernist cares about big things, like whales, more than little things, like fetuses; big things like governments, more than little things like families and neighborhoods; big things like states, which last hundreds of years, more than little things like souls, which last forever.

Thus, a modernist is one who puts his faith and hope for progress in precisely the one thing that cannot progress: matter. A traditionalist, on the other hand, is one who "looks not to the things that are seen but to the things that are unseen, for the things that are seen are temporal, but the things that are unseen are eternal" (2 Cor 4:18). A traditionalist believes in "the permanent things", and "the permanent things" cannot progress because they are the things to which all real progress progresses.

Perhaps I should modify my stark statement that matter cannot progress at all. Perhaps matter can progress, but only with and in and for spirit. If your body and your tools and your possessions serve your spirit, make you truly happy and good and wise, they contribute to progress, too.

But this modification does not help the progressive at all, since it is pretty obvious that modernity's technological know-how and power have not made us happier, wiser, better, or more saintly than our ancestors. When we speak of modern progress, we do not mean progress in happiness, in contentment, in peace of mind. Nor do we mean progress in holiness and moral perfection or wisdom. We speak readily of "modern knowledge" but never of "modern wisdom". Rather, we speak of "ancient wisdom". For wisdom is to knowledge what *kairos* is to *kronos:* the spiritual and purposive and teleological and moral dimension.

Incidentally, this point about *kairos* and *kronos* liberates us not only from the ignorant worship of the nonexistent god "progress" but also from the ignorant lust to be "up-to-date". A date, being mere *kronos,* has no character. It is almost nothing. It is a one-dimensional line, the circumference. A line can have no color. Only *kairos,* only a two-dimensional segment of the circle, can have character, and color. Since a date is only a point on the circumference, it has no character. Nothing can ever be really "up-to-date". What a wild-goose chase is our lust to be "with it" or "contemporary"! What a waste of passion and love and energy!

It's all in the Bible, of course. All this stuff about "love not the world" and how hard it is for the rich to be saved—it's very practical. Saint Teresa of Avila wrote, "Anyone who wishes to enter the second Mansion will be well advised, as far as his state of life permits, to try to put aside all unnecessary affairs and business." One thing painfully obvious about modern progress is that we all are much busier now than we ever used to be. All these time-saving devices have done exactly the opposite of saving time: they've killed time, or enslaved us to time, to *kronos,* to the clock. Jesus is a very good psychologist when he says, in the parable of the sower, that we are choked and suffocated by the brambles of the cares and riches and pleasures of life, so the seed of life cannot grow, cannot progress. Progress retards progress! Progress is the enemy of progress! Business chokes our real business here. Riches make real riches extremely difficult. Remember Mother Teresa's simple, Christlike words at Harvard: "You did not invite me here from a poor country to speak to a rich country. America is not a rich country. America is a desperately spiritually poor country." America is a poor country. This only seems paradoxical to us. In fact, it is simplicity itself. It is we who are standing on our heads; that's why Christ's simplicities appear to us as upside-down paradoxes. Once we get right side up again, we will see how simple it is. And the world will see *us* as upside down and strange, and "out of it". How wonderful to be "out of it" when "it" is the maelstrom.

You may doubt the paradoxical point that progress retards progress. You may think it too pessimistic, world-denying, anti-progressive, irrelevant—"out of it", in a word. Well, here is one more argument for my outrageous paradox against progress. Let's take modernity's supposed progress to its limit, its end, its success. I think its failure will be most clearly and spectacularly evident if we look at its supreme success, by its own standards—like a prosecuting attorney who simply lets the accused criminal talk on and on and hang himself.

Modernity's progress in conquering nature is incomplete because nature still holds one trump card over all her conquerors: death. Nature always has the last word. Suppose genetic engineering conquered death. That would be the supreme triumph. Or would it?

Let's backtrack to Eden. You remember the story, of course. It began with Satan's invention of the world's oldest profession, advertising: "Eat this; it will make you like God." It was a lie, of course, like most of the industry. Modern technology is Satan's new advertisement. It tempts us, as it tempted Eve, to become like God in power (but not in virtue). Artificial immortality would be the supreme sell-job. We would mortgage our soul for that, the conquest of the very power of life. That would conquer even the cherubim whom God stationed at the gate of Eden with a flaming sword to prevent us from eating the fruit of the tree of eternal life.

Death was God's severe mercy, the tourniquet around the wound of sin, to limit sin to eighty years or so. Remove the tourniquet, and history would bleed to death. Imagine the Roman Empire forever. Imagine the Third Reich forever. Imagine America forever. Lewis speaks of our "nightmare civilizations" whirling around themselves in never-ending gyrations of selfishness and despair (in *Miracles*), and (elsewhere, in *Mere Christianity*) of eggs that never hatched (by death) and so went rotten. "You can't just be a good egg forever; you must hatch or go bad." Death lets us hatch; artificial immortality would make us go bad forever. Hell incarnate would reign on earth. That would have to be the end of the world. And most geneticists estimate we will have it in two to three hundred years (according to Osborn Seagerberg in *The Immortality Factor*).

Let's now back up and ask the psychological question about motivation: Why did our civilization suddenly develop this lust for power? What caused the great sea change that *The Abolition of Man* defines? Why did we get a new *summum bonum,* "man's conquest of Nature", or power?

I think Nietzsche, of all people, provides us with the answer. The children of this world are wiser in their own generation than the children of light. Nietzsche, the prophet of nihilism, understands modern nihilism better than its critics sometimes. Here is the sentence in Nietzsche that answers our question. Viktor Frankl quotes it in *Man's Search for Meaning* as the key to why some survived the Nazi death camps and others, often the strongest, did not: "A man can endure almost any *how* if only he has a *why.*" In other words, you can endure bad circumstances, powerlessness, poverty, even a concentration camp, if and only if you have a meaning and purpose to your whole life, and therefore also to suffering, which is part of life. The corollary is that if you do *not* have a "why", you will not be able to endure any "how" that is a little upsetting.

This explains the origin of modern technology. It did not drop out of the sky. Nor did mankind suddenly get smart by some genetic mutation. Rather, the old "why", the old *summum bonum,* began to weaken and decay. Once the sense of life's significance was lost, we could not endure its sufferings, so we *had* to invent ways of conquering nature to reduce those sufferings radically. A man with no "why" *must* conquer his "how".

Saint Thomas Aquinas says, "No man can live without delight. That is why a man deprived of spiritual joy goes over to carnal pleasures." The same is true of societies as of individuals. When "God is dead", idols must be worshipped, for man is innately a worshipper. When true joy dies, false joys must be believed in. We are addicts. That's the only explanation for the amazing fact that the whole human race idiotically tries the same experiment over and over again, with endless little variations, even though it has failed every single time, billions and billions of times: the experiment of idolatry, of hoping to find happiness and joy and fulfillment and adequate and final meaning in this world, trying to find the *summum bonum* in the creature rather than the Creator. In light of the dismal track record of this vehicle, it is amazing that we keep gassing it up and putting it on the road again. It is more than amazing—it is insanity. The human race is spiritually insane. That is what the shocking doctrine of Original Sin means. It is shocking to us only because we are standing on our heads again, just as with the paradox about progress.

True joy is significance; false joy is power. True joy is finding truth and choosing goodness and beauty. False joy is fabricating ideologies and "creating your own values" and buying beauty. True joy is smelling the rose; false joy is plucking and possessing it.

Western civilization began to worship power when it began to doubt significance. The reason Lewis, Chesterton, Williams, Tolkien, and Thomas Howard fascinate us so much is that they still live in the medieval world, a world chock-full of built-in, God-designed significance. That's why they all think analogically, sacramentally, imagistically. For them, everything means something beyond itself.

Everything is not only a thing, but a sign, full of significance. Modernity, confining itself to the scientific method as the model for knowing reality, deliberately induces in itself what Lewis calls a dog-like state of mind, full of facts and empty of significance. Point to your dog's food and he will sniff your finger. Show a baby a book and he will try to eat it rather than read it. Show modern man a lion and he will try to tame it and make money out of it in a circus, and smile superiorly at the quaint old medievals who saw it as the King of Beasts and the natural symbol in the animal kingdom of the great King of Kings.

That's also why modern Scripture scholars tend to be either fundamentalist literalists or modernist demythologizers: neither side sees that an event like the Resurrection can be both a literal historical fact and a sign or symbol. The words man makes are signs that point to things beyond themselves; but the things God makes are also signs. The whole world points beyond itself. But the whole modern mind has lost this sign-reading dimension of consciousness. Even Christians have to strain to see it. We have lost the very powerful and all-pervasive sense of significance; therefore we must replace it with science (i.e., factual knowledge) and technology (i.e., power).

At the far end of this loss of significance lies Deconstructionism, which denies that even words have significance, intentionality, a meaning that points beyond themselves. Archibald MacLeish says, "A poem must be palpable and mute, / Like globed fruit . . . a poem must not mean, but be." If this means what it seems to mean, it is proto-deconstructionism, linguistic nihilism, and the beginning of the end—the end of a human history and consciousness that begins with "In the beginning was the Word." Nietzsche wrote, sagely, "We [i.e., we atheists] are not done with God until we are done with grammar." It looks like we are now beginning to be done with grammar. The next step can be clearly seen by reading the apotheosis of *That Hideous Strength,* the Babel scene, or its original in Genesis 11 and Revelation 18. The ancient Tower of Babel story in Genesis and the apocalyptic Fall of Babylon prophecy in Revelation are the spiritual meaning of modernity. These two chapters are mirrors, reflecting each other and ourselves.

We're almost finished. We've spent nearly all our time on the diagnosis, and now we have to make a very quick prognosis and prescription, the last two of our four steps in our spiritual medical analysis of Western civilization.

The diagnosis was very bad news indeed. I wish it were not. Honestly, I do not enjoy playing the part of the prophet of doom. Like most Americans, I like to be liked, and the messenger of bad news is seldom liked. Do you like your dentist when he tells you your roots are decayed? I fear many of you will remember only one thing from this chapter years hence: Kreeft is a Puddleglum. Doom and gloom loom on his horizon.

Actually, I *am* a Puddleglum. (The Boston Red Sox have taught me that Calvinistic, New England wisdom.) Yet my prognosis is surprisingly optimistic. For seven reasons, I will not pronounce the patient dead yet, or even terminal.

First, ignorance. No one knows the future but God.

Second, free will. Repentance, turning back, has happened in history and can happen again. If the liberal claims to have a bright crystal ball, the conservative shouldn't claim to have a dark one, but none at all. The liberal believes in maximal external freedom because he does not really believe in the primary internal freedom, free will, and the moral responsibility that goes with it, a responsibility that extends even to our eternal destiny. We who believe in free will must never despair of the salvation of any soul (remember the thief on the cross) or any society (remember ancient Israel).

Third, there is the "skin of our teeth" principle. Humanity always seems to survive by the skin of its teeth (to use the point and title of an old Thornton Wilder play). If any one of a thousand chances had gone just slightly the other way, none of us would be here now. If the temperature of the primeval fireball had been a trillionth of a degree hotter or colder three seconds after the Big Bang, no life could ever have evolved anywhere in the universe. If the cosmic rays had not bombarded the primeval slime at just the right angle, protein molecules could never have come out of the stew. If Europe had not invented ale before the Black Death polluted the water supply, most of our ancestors would have died. If Hitler had gotten the atom bomb, he would have destroyed the world. If your grandfather hadn't turned his head right instead of left one day and noticed your grandmother on the trolley, he would never have dated her, married her, and begat you. If one Egyptian tailor hadn't cheated on the threads of Joseph's mantle, Potiphar's wife would never have been able to tear it, present it as evidence to Potiphar that Joseph attacked her, gotten him thrown into prison, and let him be in a position to interpret Pharaoh's dream, win his confidence, advise him to store seven years of grain, and save his family, the seventy original Jews from whom Jesus came. We owe our salvation to a cheap Egyptian tailor.

Fourth, there is the rebound principle. After each night, a day. After each trough, a wave. Eclipses end. Communism is dying. Bad things die. American decadence will die. If necessary, America will die, too. Diseases run their course. If our civilization is doomed, mankind is not—not till the end of the world, and that's the happiest event of all, the coming of our Bridegroom. *Maranatha!*

Fifth, the Church is now the counterculture, not the culture, not the fat-cat establishment; a catacomb church, not a Constantinian church. The Church thrives in every place she is persecuted—Poland, Lithuania, East Germany, China. She is sick only where she is established: England, West Germany, Holland, Scandinavia. What an exciting change of battle plans our General is now overseeing: from defense to offense! We are now spies, guerrillas. *We* are the barbarians at the gates.

Sixth, the Church *will* win. Christ *will* win. That is guaranteed, by the only absolutely trustworthy Guarantor there is. If we only remember where our true country and our true citizenship lie, we are absolutely certain of victory. All who seek Christ find him. If that is not so, then he is a liar and you don't *want* to find him.

Seventh, the strongest force in history is not man's sin but God's grace. "Where sin abounded, grace did much more abound" (Rom 5:20). God can't lose. Othello can lose to Iago, but Shakespeare can't lose. God is our Shakespeare. History is his story. Identify with our Author and you can't lose either in the end.

But that's only "in the end". That's the long-range prognosis. What of the short-range prognosis for that little local pocket of stuff called modern Western civilization? That may be another kettle of fish entirely. The fish may be so rotten that the only thing for God to do is to throw it out. And would that be so terrible, really? Compared with what we've just looked at, compared with the Church and compared with the grace of God, the survival of Western civilization is a triviality. Our civilization is a carbuncle on the cosmos, a hemorrhoid on history.

Finally, the prescription: What shall we do? How shall we fight the good fight? What are our marching orders as we prepare for Armageddon, or Marathon, or Waterloo?

Four answers come to mind, four practical principles, four prescriptions.

First, be counter-cultural. Like the Bible. Like the early Church. Like Augustine's *City of God.* Like Jesus. "Be not conformed to this world, but be transformed by the renewing of your minds." Be a nut, a fanatic, a weirdo. Was it ever said of the early Christians that they were "cool", or "with it"? Or, to use exact adult equivalents, that they were "appropriate" or "acceptable"? No, here's what the world said: "These that have turned the world upside down have come here" (Acts 17:6). Let's turn the world upside down, for it's standing on its head.

Second, be ready. Be ready for battle, for we are at war. Edie Galbraith writes, in a letter to the *National Catholic Register:*

I'm getting tired of constantly praying for peace. What's wrong
with praying for *victory* once in awhile? We belong to the
Church Militant; we're engaged in a battle. The battle is with
the powers of darkness. Since there is never any shortage of
darkness, I think we should be allowed to pray for the grace to
be victorious.

What difference does it make when you think you're at war? You
get a sense of perspective. A matter of life and death appears as it
is: as a matter of life and death. Trivia appear as they are: trivia.
No one complains that the beds are lumpy on a battlefield. No
one even bleats about "sexual needs" when live bullets are whistling past the ears.

Third, be ready for the end. For we may well be very near the
end. Passionate, anxious, expectant longing for the end, for the
return of the Lord, was the high-octane fuel of the early Church.
We have watered down the fuel today.

I do not think we need to make arrogant and foolish predictions in order to say "Maranatha" with an exclamation point. A
good third baseman need not predict that the next pitch will be
hit to him as a screaming line drive in order to be prepared for
one. Let us be alert.

Alertness is not worry. Worry drains your energy; alertness
conserves it, because it is calm, not agitated: deadly calm, in the
face of a matter of life or death, especially spiritual life or death.
For the war we are all in, like it or not, is the war between Heaven
and Hell, and at stake are human souls.

Finally, for this greatest of all wars we must use the greatest of
all weapons, the strongest power that is.

Our enemies are supernatural, of course, but we also have
natural, concrete, human enemies, those who are doing Satan's
work, consciously or unconsciously, as we try to do Christ's,
those who passionately hate us and want to kill us, i.e., to destroy
the Church and make our souls like theirs. They are in the ACLU
and Planned Parenthood and the Gay and Lesbian Task Force, and

media boardrooms. But they are also in the legislatures and the universities, and sometimes even in the seminaries. What is our strongest weapon against them?

There is one that is guaranteed to defeat them, and we alone have it. Their weapon is hate, ours is love. God's love. *Agape.* We can defeat our enemies by making them our friends, by loving them to death. It may take forever. But love never ends, never gives up. Not even when it sees Calvary. And once it has seen that, everything else is trivial, including the decadence of Western civilization.

3

The Goodness of Goodness and the Badness of Badness

"The goodness of goodness and the badness of badness"—what in the world does that silly platitude mean?

Only the single most critical issue in modern history. Only the issue that is literally a matter of life or death for our civilization, our species, and our souls. Only the issue that transcends and includes such life-or-death issues as the abortion holocaust, the destruction of marriage and the family, the sodomization of civilization, endlessly spiralling rates of domestic violence, incest, child abuse, rape, suicide, drugs, and similar favorite all-American leisure occupations, as well as the likelihood of the thing *no* one seems to be worrying about any more, nuclear war. (But inner wars have a way of erupting into outer wars. Where else do wars begin? Read James 1:4.)

The overarching and overriding issue here is so big, so obvious, so simple that only farm boys and washerwomen see it—professors and professionals don't. It is the one thing you will not be taught by the "experts", i.e., the hired prostitutes of the establishment. For that would put most of them out of business. But C. S. Lewis, like the little boy in "The Emperor's New Clothes", said it loudly, clearly, and simply, in many ways, at many times, and memorably. It is the truth of the *Tao,* the news that there is a real "natural moral law". (This news has not yet reached the Democratic senators who grilled Clarence Thomas at his confirmation hearings; they were appalled that a prospective Supreme Court justice dared to believe in a real *justice.*)

Charles Malik, former President of Lebanon and of the United Nations General Assembly, put it this way:

> There is truth, and there is falsehood. There is good, and there is evil. There is happiness, and there is misery. There is that which ennobles, and there is that which demeans. There is that which puts you in harmony with yourself, with others, with the universe, and with God, and there is that which alienates you from yourself, from the world, and from God. These things are different and separate and totally distinguishable from one another. Truth is not the same as falsehood, happiness is not the same as misery.
>
> The greatest error in modern times is the confusion between these orders. Nothing is anything firm in itself—this is the great heresy of the modern world. But there is no power on earth or in heaven that can make falsehood truth, evil good, misery happiness, slavery freedom. And yet what do philosophers tell you in the great centers of learning? They insist that everything depends on what you mean. The mind becomes so blurred and blunted in its judgment that it fails to see the real, given distinction between things.
>
> How do we become true and good, happy and genuine, joyful and free? Only by getting in touch with good, true, happy, genuine human beings. Read the Psalms and the Gospels reverently and prayerfully every day, and I guarantee you two things: first, that you will experience in your own life and being a taste of what is beautiful and strong and certain and free; and second, you will then develop a sharpness of vision to differentiate between the true and the phony, between the beautiful and the hideous, between the noble and the mean.

Arnold Toynbee distinguished twenty-one great civilizations in human history; other historians number hundreds. Not one of these has ever survived or thrived without belief in the *Tao,* in the goodness of goodness and the badness of badness. But the philosophy presently ensconced in power and accelerating in arrogance and intolerance in our civilization is one that scorns and sneers at this universal human philosophy as "judgmental", "simplistic", and "oppressive". We are living in the middle of a gigantic social science laboratory experiment in moral denial. We are playing elaborate intellectual games on the deck of the *Titanic.*

Civilizations all die anyway, sooner or later, of course, just like individuals. To die is no disgrace; to have lived in vain is disgrace. Lewis reminds us of a primary platitude in "First and Second Things": that if survival is our *summum bonum* — if life itself is all we live for — then we certainly will not survive. Civilizations, like individuals, survive only if they have a goal, an end, a purpose beyond mere living and surviving, something *for* which to live and survive. A civilization that believes in nothing worth dying for will surely and ignobly die.

We are obviously living amid just such a civilization. What can we do, we who live amid the morally insane? What can we do with those who have unlearned even the very first and simplest lesson of moral kindergarten, "the goodness of goodness and the badness of badness"?

We can and must fight. Spiritually, of course, not physically; for "we wrestle not against flesh and blood but against principalities and powers." We must wake up and smell the corpses and realize that we are on a battlefield, like it or not. In this warfare, there are two kinds of weapons. Lewis can help us only a little with one kind, but a lot with the other.

The strongest weapon is sanctity: suffering love and persistent prayer. These are like battleship guns, or bombing runs. But we also need intellectual weapons, arguments. These are like M-1s, infantry rifles. Here Lewis can help us very much.

In this chapter I want to take an inventory of the M-1s in Lewis' arsenal, to equip you for battle, to provide you with intellectual weapons that will not break in your hands or in your mouth or in your mind when you use them. Refusing such weapons today when you live in academia or journalism is like refusing a suit of armor and a sword when you walk across Central Park in New York City at night because they are too old-fashioned.

Lewis refuted no fewer than twenty moral heresies, twenty different denials of the "goodness of goodness and the badness of badness". They are either substitutes for the *Tao* or *Tao*-less systems, either new *Taos* or No *Taos*. They are:

1. Subjectivism: the subjectivity of goodness and badness;

2. Emotivism (one of subjectivism's little brothers): the reduction of goodness and badness to emotions;

3. Positivism (another of subjectivism's little brothers): the idea that man posits values with his will, invents goodness and badness;

4. Cultural relativism, or conventionalism: the relativity of goodness and badness to place, or culture;

5. Historicism: the relativity of goodness and badness to time;

6. Utilitarianism: the reduction of goodness to utility, or efficiency;

7. Instinctualism: the reduction of goodness to biological instinct;

8. Hedonism: the reduction of goodness to pleasure;

9. Egotism: the reduction of goodness to enlightened selfishness;

10. Pragmatism: the weakness of goodness and the power of badness;

11. Optimistic humanism: the denial of the existence of human badness;

12. Cynicism: the denial of the existence of human goodness;

13. Pop-psychobabble: the niceness of goodness and the nastiness of badness;

14. Moral philistinism: the dullness of goodness and the beauty of badness;

15. Rationalism: the simplicity and plainness of goodness;

16. Calvinism: the reduction of goodness to arbitrary divine decree;

17. Secularism: the reduction of goodness to the merely horizontal (human);

18. Pantheism: the identity of goodness and badness;

19. Moralism: the idolization of moral goodness as ultimate;

20. Nietzscheanism: the goodness of badness and the badness of goodness, the "transvaluation of all values".

1. Subjectivism

The master heresy is subjectivism. It is the parent of all the others, for only after the objective truth is denied are we "free" to recreate new "truths" in the image of our own desires. Only when we fall asleep to the real world are we "free" to dream nightmare worlds into being.

Lewis dissects subjectivism especially in *The Abolition of Man,* surely his most terrifying, prophetic, and apocalyptically important book; in book 1 of *Mere Christianity;* and in "The Poison of Subjectivism" (in *Christian Reflections*). In the latter article, he stated the radical nature of subjectivism thus:

Until modern times no thinker of the first rank ever doubted that our judgements of value were rational judgements or that what they discovered was objective. . . . The modern view is very different. It does not believe that value judgements are really judgements at all. They are sentiments, or complexes, or attitudes, produced in a community . . . and differing from one community to another. To say that a thing is good is merely to express our feeling about it; and our feeling about it is the feeling we have been socially conditioned to have.

But if this is so, then we might have been conditioned to feel otherwise. 'Perhaps,' thinks the reformer or the educational expert, 'it would be better if we were. Let us improve our morality.' Out of this apparently innocent idea comes the disease that will certainly end our species (and, in my view, damn our souls) if it is not crushed: the fatal superstition that men can create values.

Part 1 of *Mere Christianity* offers three arguments from common and verifiable experience against moral subjectivism and for the objective reality of the moral law.

The first is the observation that people *quarrel.* They have moral *arguments;* they do not merely *fight,* as animals do. They try to justify their behavior by appealing to a moral law, or standard. Everyone in the world does this except the subjectivist (and even he usually forgets himself and slips into moral language). If he is right, everyone else who has ever lived has been radically and inexplicably wrong, has been using words as meaningless as a child's fantasies about an invisible playmate (which is how they usually see religious language, too). In other words, to be a subjectivist you have to be a snob.

A second argument shows that you also have to be a hypocrite. The subjectivist does not live subjectivism, does not practice what he preaches; for when you treat him unjustly, he protests that you are being unjust, or unfair. No relativist acts like a relativist when he is being victimized. He is eager to claim the status of victim.

(Actually, many psychologists teach a consistent and total

subjectivism. They teach you that you should never say "ought" or "should" or "wrong", only "I feel". When someone hurts you, say, "You know, I feel very hurt by that." A very convenient philosophy for muggers. I have yet to hear a psychologist dare to preach it to a rape victim.)

Lewis' third argument is that most people think that one morality (e.g., a democratic, tolerant morality) is really better than another (e.g., a Nazi, intolerant morality). Thus they appeal to a real standard overarching and judging the subjective beliefs or feelings of democrats and Nazis alike. Even if a subjectivist refrains from making this natural appeal, he almost always believes in moral "progress"—the "progress" from the traditional, "unenlightened", objectivist morality to the modern, "enlightened", subjectivist morality. But progress implies a real, objective standard to judge it as progress rather than regress. Progress means not just change but change for the better.

Lewis' conclusion is simply two truths from moral kindergarten:

> First, that human beings, all over the earth, have this curious idea that they ought to behave in a certain way, and cannot really get rid of it. Secondly, that they do not in fact behave in that way. They know the Law of Nature; they break it. These two facts are the foundation for all clear thinking about ourselves and the universe we live in.

The typically modern professor or expert is one who denies these two facts. That is the fundamental reason why Chicken Little was right.

2. Emotivism

Two derivative forms of this master heresy of subjectivism are emotivism and positivism. Emotivism is the soft form; positivism, the hard form. The hard form is more fearsome than the soft, but the soft paves the way for it. Ultimately, the hard form—the view that man's will posits values—led to the Nazi death camps, just as it led Dostoyevsky's Raskalnikov to murder and Ivan Karamazov to insanity. But the gentle, innocent-sounding, "liberal", "tolerant" moral dogma that moral dogmas are only feelings laid the tracks for the train that took us to Auschwitz. The man-serving dogma became a man-eating dog.

Lewis refutes emotivism in *The Abolition of Man* by

> the well-known story of Coleridge at the waterfall. You remember that there were two tourists present: that one called it 'sublime' and the other 'pretty'; and that Coleridge mentally endorsed the first judgement and rejected the second with disgust.... [The emotivist authors Lewis criticizes] comment as follows: 'When the man said *That is sublime,* he appeared to be making a remark about the waterfall.... Actually ... he was not making a remark about the waterfall, but a remark about his own feelings.'

But, Lewis notes,

> the view ... would lead to obvious absurdities. It would force them to maintain that *You are contemptible* means *I have contemptible feelings:* in fact that *Your feelings are contemptible* means *My feelings are contemptible.*

But the real refutation is that subjectivism distorts what we *mean:*

> The man who called the cataract sublime was not intending simply to describe his own emotions about it: he was also claiming that the object was one which *merited* those emotions. But for this claim there would be nothing to agree or disagree about. To disagree with *This is pretty* if those words simply described the lady's feelings, would be absurd: if she had said *I feel sick* Coleridge would hardly have replied *No, I feel quite well.*

If emotivism is true, then, as Lewis puts it in *Miracles,* "*I ought* is the same sort of statement as *I itch.*"

3. Positivism

If man freely posits or creates moral values with his will, rather than unfreely standing under them and discovering them with his moral reason, or conscience, then the value-creators stand outside values. They "condition" values in other men. They are Supermen, the "Conditioners", and their patients are the "conditioned". The overall argument in chapter 3 of *The Abolition of Man* sends a chill up your spine when you realize (1) how logically inevitable the analysis is, and (2) how socially accurate the description is. The wildly wide gap between the values, or lack of values, of our present Conditioners, the media elite (see Michael Medved, *Hollywood versus America*), and ordinary people means we are well on the road to the "abolition of man", e.g., 72 percent of ordinary people believe abortion is somehow a bad thing and should be somehow restricted, but only 3 percent of the elite do. Over 90 percent believe it is wrong to cheat on your spouse, to commit adultery; less than 50 percent of the elite do. Over 50 percent attend religious services; 9 percent of the elite do.

Lewis' argument *against* these moral "Conditioners" is simple. It is the self-contradiction of "the moral reformer who, after saying that 'good' means 'what we are conditioned to like', goes on cheerfully to consider whether it might be 'better' that we should be conditioned to like something else. What in Heaven's name does he mean by 'better'?" (*Letters*). If you stand outside and above the moral law, if you posit rather than discover values, you cannot be good or do good; you are beyond good and evil. You are playing God. You are not even a bad man. You are not a man at all. You are an orc, a troll, a *golem.*

4. Cultural Relativism

There are two arguments here that Lewis refutes. First, the argument that the moral law is conditioned in us by our society, i.e., parents and teachers. But what is conditioned in us by society is subjective and man-made. Therefore, the moral law is subjective and man-made.

Lewis simply notes that the second premise is false. Some things we learn from parents and teachers are conventional, like our native language or the rules of the road, but others are natural, universal, and objective, like the laws of mathematics, or geography.

The second argument is that if different cultures have radically different values, then values are man-made. Different cultures have radically different values. Therefore, values are man-made.

In this argument, *both* premises are false. First, even if two different cultures disagreed totally about values, one could be right and one wrong, just as they could be about anything else they disagree about. In fact, the fact that they disagree and argue and quarrel shows that each thinks it is objectively right; neither culture believes in cultural relativism. Why is it unthinkable to dare to be so politically incorrect as to believe that cultures, like individuals, are not morally infallible? Probably because the only religious absolute left in the modern American relativist is the dogma that no idea, philosophy, or culture can ever be superior to any other. This idea itself is self-contradictory, of course, since it pits modern culture, which believes this nonsense, against all ancient cultures, which disbelieve it, and declares us superior. Would that we would be really multicultural; we would learn from the moral absolutism of all other cultures in the history of the world except our own. Our cultural relativism is really the most arrogant kind of cultural imperialism and elitism.

The second premise of the argument is also false: cultures do *not* differ radically about values. As Lewis shows in the Appendix to *The Abolition of Man,* there is strong agreement across cultures on basic values; there is empirical evidence for a universally known natural moral law. What culture has ever valued lying, cowardice, theft, murder, injustice, or selfishness and disvalued veracity, courage, justice, respect for life, and unselfishness? The most radical exception is probably modern culture, which at least has disvalued chastity, fidelity, and also piety: three things valued by almost all previous cultures. (The question, of course, is not how well cultures have lived up to their values, but what values they have professed. They may not have practiced what they preached, but the only reason we do is because we preach no more.)

5. Historicism

Goodness no more changes with time than it changes with space, geography, or culture. Historicism says it does. (Hegel is the main villain here.) The historicist often silences proposals to arrest our moral decay with the cliché "you can't turn back the clock." Lewis, remembering his Chesterton, replies (in *Mere Christianity,* chapter 5) simply that you *can.* When the clock goes wrong, that is exactly what you do, unless you are its slave. Instead of being master of time and servant of truth, modern man thinks he is the master of truth and the servant of time—an illustration of the law that if you will not worship the true God, you will inevitably bow before some silly idol.

The argument that "you can't turn back the clock" is very similar to the argument you always hear for fornication (and condoms) and abortion: "They're going to do it anyway" (frequently followed by "you can't turn back the clock"). This is an argument that is never given for anything unconnected with sex. Try giving it for racism, rape, or even smoking, and you will see how logical and consistent it is.

Probably the clearest example of a historicist in Lewis' fiction is Weston, in *Perelandra.* Remember his philosophical dialogue with Ransom about Emergent Evolution? Please remember how that dialogue ended, how Lewis unmasked the demonic identity of the Zeitgeist, the Spirit of the Times.

The reference to damnation is deliberate. According to the Bible, to be saved you must first repent. This is the one thing a historicist progressivist assures us we cannot do: turn back, turn back the clock.

I should confine my quotations to Lewis, but I cannot resist quoting Tolkien here against the historicist. There is a passage in *The Lord of the Rings* that rings out with liberty like a trumpet to the modern reader who has been taught nothing but the slavery to Historicism. Eomer meets Aragorn most unexpectedly, and says:

> "It is hard to be sure of anything among so many marvels. The world is all grown strange. Elf and Dwarf in company walk in our daily fields; and folk speak with the Lady of the Wood and yet live; and the Sword comes back to war that was broken. . . . How shall a man judge what to do in such times?"
>
> "As he ever has judged," said Aragorn. "Good and evil have not changed since yesteryear, nor are they one thing among Elves and Dwarves and another among Men. It is a man's part to discern them, as much in the Golden Wood as in his own house."

6. Utilitarianism

Utilitarianism claims to have found a purely naturalistic substitute for the *Tao* in utility to the community. Justice and charity work; injustice and selfishness do not. That's all there is, there ain't no more.

Lewis sees the logical problem with utilitarianism this way: to say you should practice self-sacrifice because unless some practice this, the community will not thrive or survive, is true, but this assumes that the community *should* thrive or survive; why? The argument derives an "ought" from an "is", value from fact, the moral goodness of self-sacrifice from its factual utility. There is more in the conclusion than in the premise. You need a moral premise to get a moral conclusion. (This is the nub of his critique in chapter 2 of *The Abolition of Man.*)

There is a further problem in Utilitarianism. Granted that unless some work for others, all will be harmed; why should I be the one? Why should I put others ahead of myself? Why shouldn't I put myself ahead of others and the community? The only answer is the *Tao:* because it's wrong. Utilitarianism, which sets out to displace the *Tao,* needs the *Tao* to justify its own premises.

7. Instinctualism

The second substitute for the *Tao* which Lewis considers in *The Abolition of Man* — instinct — fares no better than the first one. There may indeed be a herd instinct, leading us to work for others; but why should we follow it? Again, "ought" is derived from "is", value from fact, more from less.

In *Mere Christianity,* Lewis gives three refutations of the claim that morality is just another animal instinct. First, instinct is a different kind of feeling from moral obligation: "Feeling a desire to help is quite different from feeling that you ought to help whether you want to or not." Second, our instincts are often in conflict, so if morality were merely instinct, and there were nothing else in us — no transcendent conscience to judge instincts — then the strongest instinct would always win. But it often does not. We sometimes risk danger and help the drowning man or the old lady being mugged, in the teeth of our strongest instinct, self-preservation. Third, "if the moral law were one of our instincts, we ought to be able to point to some one impulse inside us which was always what we call 'good' . . . but you cannot." Instincts are like piano keys, morality like sheet music: the standard which judges from above which keys are right to play at what time.

8. Hedonism

Hedonism identifies the good with pleasure. Lewis does not deny that pleasure is good (actually, it is old Screwtape who denies that!). Pleasure is good, but goodness is not the same as pleasure.

Respectable hedonism is social hedonism. It does not ask virtue, only sharing your vices. It does not require you to build strength of character, just to share your pleasant weaknesses with others. A mere "Golden Rule" ethic, a mere "love your neighbor" ethic (which is all we ever hear from our liberal pulpits) is quite compatible with hedonism. The Golden Rule would forbid murder, theft, and lying, but not adultery; that is why it is so popular. "Do unto others as you would have them do unto you"—and many would be very happy to be seduced, therefore they seduce.

Lewis' last published work before he died was prophetically and providentially aimed at our most life-changing revolution, the sexual revolution. Its title says it all: "We Have No 'Right to Happiness' ". In pursuing happiness, even if we are shallow enough to identify it with pleasure, and even if we are restrictive enough to mean only sexual pleasure, we do not have the right to lie, cheat, steal, betray, and harm. This is the moral essence of the sexual revolution: "The sexual motive is taken to condone all sorts of behavior which, if it had any other end in view, would be condemned as merciless, treacherous, and unjust."

9. Egotism, or Enlightened Selfishness

A variant on hedonism is calculating egotism: the view that morality is merely convenience, or what pays. It takes only a little rational enlightenment to realize that if we stop killing each other, we will all be happier. Why must morality be any more than that? Morality pays. The tribe that stopped bashing each other's brains out survived, and we evolved and learned from them.

But, as Lewis argues in *Mere Christianity,* "a man occupying the corner seat in the train because he got there first, and a man who slipped into it while my back was turned and removed my bag, are both equally inconvenient. But I blame the second man and do not blame the first." Thus morality is not simply convenience, or what pays.

There is a religious version of this egotistic mistake, which Lewis also refutes in *Mere Christianity*. It sees morality as a deal with God: if we obey his rules, he will give us pleasure as reward (whether in this life or the next). This misses the whole point of morality: "We might think that God wanted simply obedience to a set of rules, whereas he really wants people of a particular sort." Morality is a necessity to transform our character to make us the kind of people that can endure and enjoy Heaven. For (as Lewis shows in the transcendently beautiful chapter on Heaven in *The Problem of Pain*) the essence of Heaven is participation in the trinitarian life of self-giving love. Morality is not respectable, enlightened egotism; it is more like an operation, or rather life after the operation, which is the "new birth" or the beginning of divine life in us.

> For in self-giving . . . we touch a rhythm not only of all creation but of all being. . . . From the highest [God] to the lowest, self exists to be abdicated, and, by that abdication, becomes the more truly self, to be thereupon yet the more abdicated, and so forever. This is not a heavenly law which we can escape by remaining earthly, nor an earthly law which we can escape by being saved. What is outside the system of self-giving is not earth, nor nature, nor 'ordinary life' but simply and solely Hell.

10. Pragmatism

Pragmatism, in the popular rather than the technical, philosophical sense, believes in the weakness of goodness and the power of badness and therefore counsels a bit of badness. "The end justifies the means." The Sophists, Machiavelli, and Mao Tse-tung (who defined justice as "something that comes out of the barrel of a gun") were pragmatists. Uncle Andrew in *The Magician's Nephew* and the N.I.C.E. in *That Hideous Strength* are pragmatists. Ironically, this practical and this-worldly philosophy usually seems to get involved in the demonic, as in the previous examples. The realism of such cautionary tales would seem to be adequate refutation of pragmatism. We don't need sophisticated philosophical arguments to know Machiavelli isn't a good guy. But we may need philosophers and novelists to convince us that the pragmatic premise is false: badness isn't stronger than goodness. Villains are *weak* men. Plato took ten books, in *The Republic,* to prove that "justice is always more profitable than injustice." But a good novelist needs only realistic characters to convince us of this.

11. Optimistic Humanism

We could label this heresy "the nonexistence of badness". It is Rousseau's idea of man as "noble savage" and puts all the blame on "the system," not on man (as if "the system" came from demons, not men). For the humanist, only one Catholic dogma is true: the Immaculate Conception—but it is true of everyone.

Like the previous heresy, this dreamy absurdity needs no elaborate argument to refute it. As Chesterton said, the dogma of Original Sin is the only Christian dogma that is empirically verifiable just by reading daily newspapers. The spiritual warfare in *That Hideous Strength,* similar to the one in the Book of Revelation, is utterly realistic, and we recognize this plot in every story, or nearly every story, that we tell. For what is any plot but the story of good versus evil?

In *Perelandra,* the evil is so real that Ransom is commanded by Maleldil to *kill* Weston, the "un-man", the Devil's vehicle. God seems to have commanded the same sort of thing frequently in the Old Testament without taking polls of the shocked sensibilities of humanistic pacifists. (We may also refer the reader to Lewis' address to the Pacifist Society, "Why I Am Not a Pacifist". And, of course, to the chapter "Human Wickedness" in *The Problem of Pain.*)

12. Cynicism

Optimistic Humanism denies the existence of badness; pessimistic Cynicism denies the existence of goodness. Like pragmatism, both are equally refuted by experience, by lived story. The Dwarfs in *The Last Battle* are examples of cynics. You will note the exact parallel between Lewis' description of the Dwarfs and his description of Hell in *The Problem of Pain.* Both are states of closed-minded, closed-hearted refusals to trust and to believe. One needs no argument to refute misery.

Puddleglum (in *The Silver Chair*), by the way, is not a cynic. He is a moralist. He believes in spiritual warfare, unlike both the denier of evil and the denier of good. But he also believes in Murphy's law. (Murphy was a Red Sox fan.)

13. Pop-Psychobabble

Please excuse the barbaric coinage, but this position deserves the ugliest insult inventable. It is the identification of goodness with niceness and badness with nastiness. In other words, this morality is almost as mature as "Mister Rogers' Neighborhood". Its favorite slogans are "compassion" (especially in the mouths of politicians who want to play Dracula to you) and "nonjudgmentalism" (especially in the mouths of the most judgmental people in the world, who want to remove your freedom to speak moral platitudes by calling them "bigotry").

The origin of this moral tapioca was diagnosed by Chesterton when he said that when a man has lost all his moral principles, he still believes in compassion. These people are also always saying that ethical decisions are very complex—which is a simple lie.

Nearly all ethical decisions are clear and simple, except to someone with no principles. The *Tao* is not a puzzle for scholars but a light for travelers.

Lewis' distinction between Goodness and Kindness in *The Problem of Pain* and the character of Aslan in the Chronicles of Narnia—Aslan, who is "not safe. But he's good"—refutes this confusion between goodness and niceness. As Rabbi Abraham Heschel said, "God is not nice. God is not an uncle. God is an earthquake."

14. Moral Philistinism

I mean by this title the heresy of the dullness of goodness and the beauty of badness. It is the Devil's first lie, and it is his most successful. Lewis is one of the very few modern novelists who have not succumbed to it. (Tolkien and Charles Williams are two others.) How many can portray good as more interesting than evil, heroes as more interesting than villains? How many have heroes at all?

Hannah Arendt saw through this illusion in *Eichmann in Jerusalem,* where she spoke of "the banality of evil". The Nazis were an example of it, like the N.I.C.E. in *That Hideous Strength:* they seemed fascinating from a distance but up close proved to be only tedious, shallow, boring, and ugly—rather like parts of New York City. (Compare its appearance from the air at night with a walk down Tenth Avenue.)

The greatest contributor to this heresy in modern times was probably Nietzsche, with his famous contrast between the "Apollonian" (the dull, rational, respectable, controlled, and ethical) and the "Dionysian" (the fascinating, irrational, rebellious, wild, and immoral). Nietzsche shared the fate of his chosen god, Dionysus, who in the Greek myth was torn apart by the Titans, the dark forces of the underworld. Nietzsche descended into insanity, and, contrary to the popular imagination, insanity is really supremely dull. The dullest place of all is Hell.

The wonderfully weird gaggle of goodfolk at St. Anne's in *That Hideous Strength* refute the heresy of the dullness of goodness; but Lewis' supreme achievement here is surely Aslan. Who else in all of modern literature has succeeded as well in presenting Christ as a literary figure, in eliciting from the reader the same *frisson,* the same fear and trembling, awe and wonder, as Christ elicited from those who met him and continues to elicit from those who meet him in the Gospels, even in their bowdlerized, prosaic, banal modern mistranslations, and in the emasculated modern liturgies? Nothing can pull the claws of the Lion of the Tribe of Judah. And no one has kept his claws sharp on the printed page as well as Lewis. It is surely his supreme achievement on earth. I can almost hear Christ saying to Lewis what he said to Saint Thomas Aquinas after the latter had composed his profound treatise on the Eucharist: "You have written well of me, my son. What will you have as your reward?" I'm sure Lewis would have answered exactly what Saint Thomas answered: "Only Thyself, Lord."

15. Rationalism

Morality includes three dimensions, Lewis reminds us in *Mere Christianity,* while modern man usually thinks of only one. It includes social morality, individual morality (vices and virtues, character), and the question of the *summum bonum.* Like a fleet of ships, the human race needs to know not only (1) how to cooperate and not bump into each other, but also (2) how each ship is to stay afloat and shipshape, and (3) why the fleet is at sea at all, its mission. Now these last two questions are deep and metaphysical. In the words of *Till We Have Faces,* they are not "thin and clear, like water, but thick and dark, like blood". "Holy places are dark places."

The rationalist does not understand this. He thinks the good should be simple, plain, and clear to everyone. The rationalist is tempted to answer the mysterious moral question, "Why do bad things happen to good people"? as Socrates and the Stoics did: "They never do." For a good man is a wise soul, indifferent to bodily harm and in control of his own soul.

But the Priest sees more deeply and truly than the Fox. Saint Psyche suffers, apparently unjustly, and, without knowing why, she is forbidden to bring the light to her divine husband's bed. Orual cannot read this riddle right. She masks her face, trying to hide herself from the gods, and succeeds only in hiding them from her. *Till We Have Faces* shows, at least, that life's moral script is a mystery to be lived, not a puzzle to be solved. What to do is clear; the Commandments are clear; our marching orders are clear. But our divine Commander's strategy is not, and why good soldiers die young is not.

Lewis gives us part of the reason for the mystery in *Mere Christianity* when he says that morality is not merely a matter of obeying a certain set of rules, but more basically becoming a certain sort of person. The origin and end of biblical morality is: "Be ye holy *as I the Lord your God am holy.*"

It is also mysterious because it is love. *That* cannot be simple and clear because God is not simple and clear. Life is spiritual foreplay with our divine husband (we are all Psyche—soul—*and* we are all Orual—Ungit, Eve) and a good lover does not just go by the book. Instead, he writes a new book. Sometimes it is a masterpiece—like the book of Job.

16. Calvinism

Calvinism makes goodness arbitrary in making it depend solely on God's will (not his reason or his nature). Calvinism is suspicious of the *Tao,* which is known by universal moral reason and conscience. Calvinism believes that man, including his reason, is "totally depraved", therefore reason cannot be trusted to know true morality. Only faith can. With the divine will as the sole source of morality, if God wills us to murder, then murder becomes good. This is Euthyphro's "divine command theory" as opposed to Socrates' natural law theory that God does not will a thing because it is good, but a thing is good because God wills it.

Lewis argues that this Calvinism really reduces goodness to divine power and makes us ready to worship an omnipotent Fiend. Lewis explicitly rejects "total depravity" in *The Problem of Pain* and says he agrees with Socrates, Samuel Johnson, and George Macdonald against Euthyphro: God commands the good because it is good; it is not good because he commands it.

Calvinism is the extreme opposite of, and perhaps a reaction to, the rationalism that insists that goodness must always be plain and clear, and also to the secularism that tries to divorce morality from God altogether. Lewis stands between these two extremes.

17. Secularism

If Calvinism reduces morality to God's will, secularism divorces it from God entirely, and from any transcendence. This divorce, in turn, leads to the heresy of the dullness of goodness, for God is the ultimate source of all interestingness, beauty, and fascination.

Lewis refutes secularism when he uses the moral argument for the existence of God in book 1 of *Mere Christianity*. Contrary to secularism, natural morality can be traced back to God, just as second causes known by natural science can be traced back by philosophical reasoning to God as the First Cause. Both morality and the world known by science are in objective fact effects of God; but we can know the effect without knowing the cause if we do not ask ultimate philosophical questions. If we do, however, we can find God at the end of the moral clue we have been following. For an unconscious and impersonal universe cannot account for a moral law binding on my conscience.

18. Pantheism

For the pantheist, good and evil are ultimately identical, for all things are ultimately one thing, the one and only thing there is. All is one.

Against this popular pantheist idea (which, as Lewis points out in *Miracles,* is actually older and more popular than Christianity, not new and original, as it seems to modern ex-Christians), Christianity slaps us in the face with the surprising idea of "a God who takes sides, who loves love and hates hatred, who wants us to behave in one way and not another. . . . For Christianity is a fighting religion." This Christian notion of God is becoming more and more unpopular and politically incorrect. Many Christian writers, preachers, theologians, and clergy today seem to want to sail closer to the wind of pantheism than to Christianity. Orthodox Jews and Muslims seem much more battle-ready than Christians, who seem to be slip-sliding increasingly into an ecumenical orgy of New Age spiritual goo.

Lewis points out in *Mere Christianity* that there is a connection between naturalism and pantheism, between the denial of God's transcendence and the denial of the good-evil distinction. If God is not transcendent, he is equally present in everything in nature, in what we call good and in what we call evil. Hitler is a revelation of God just as Mother Teresa is. For God is just "The Force"—a sort of Blob God. He is certainly not a "he"—not a person with a will, least of all a masculine-like person ready to impregnate our souls from outside. And if God is indifferent to good and evil, we should be too once we are fully enlightened.

The conclusion of pantheism is the identification of God and the Devil. And the practical outcome of this ultimate blasphemy is seen in Weston, in *Perelandra.* After arguing with Ransom that old-fashioned moral distinctions are passé and that one era's diabolism is merely another era's progressivism (the heresy of historicism—

the heresies are connected like islands of a single undersea continent), he practices what he preaches and becomes one with The Force Beyond Good and Evil: he becomes totally demon-possessed.

This may seem harsh and extreme, but unless Christianity is false, pantheism is blasphemous and demonic, for it confuses the Holy One with the Evil One. This is more than a philosophical error; this is a demonic deception. Its origin and its end are in Hell.

19. Moralism

Kantian moralism is the heresy that morality is ultimate, superior even to religion; that man's *summum bonum* coincides with morality. The other heresies all gave to morality too little; Kantian moralism gives to morality too much.

Against this Lewis argues, in the "Hope" chapter of *Mere Christianity,* in "Man or Rabbit?", and in "The Weight of Glory", that our *summum bonum,* highest good, end, and destiny is *not* morality. Morality is the means, not the end. "The road to the Promised Land runs *past* Sinai." There are moral absolutes, but morality is not the absolute; heavenly joy and love are. In Heaven, we will look back on morality as a joke. (N.b., we are *not* in Heaven yet.)

> —I hear someone whimpering on with his question, 'Will it help me? Will it make me happy? Do you really think I'd be better if I became a Christian?' Well, if you must have it, my answer is 'Yes.' But I don't like giving an answer at all at this stage. Here is a door, behind which, according to some people, the secret of the universe is waiting for you. Either that's true, or it isn't. And if it isn't, then what the door really conceals is simply the greatest fraud, the most colossal 'sell' on record. Isn't it obviously the job of every man (that is a man and not a rabbit) to try to find out which, and then to devote his full energies either to serving this tremendous secret or to exposing and destroying this gigantic humbug? Faced with such an issue,

can you really remain wholly absorbed in your own blessed 'moral development'? . . .

Mere *morality* is not the end of life. You were made for something quite different from that. J. S. Mill and Confucius (Socrates was much nearer the reality) simply didn't know what life is about. The people who keep on asking if they can't lead a decent life without Christ, don't know what life is about; if they did they would know that 'a decent life' is mere machinery compared with the thing we men are really made for. Morality is indispensable: but the Divine Life, which gives itself to us and which calls us to be gods, intends for us something in which morality will be swallowed up. We are to be remade. All the rabbit in us is to disappear—the worried, conscientious, ethical rabbit as well as the cowardly and sensual rabbit. We shall bleat and squeal as the handfuls of fur come out; and then, surprisingly, we shall find underneath it all a thing we have never yet imagined: a real man, an ageless god, a song of God, strong, radiant, wise, beautiful, and drenched in joy. ("Man or Rabbit?")

20. Nietzschean Immoralism

Nietzsche's heresy is at the farthest possible extreme from the truth: it is the heresy of the badness of goodness and the goodness of badness—what Nietzsche called the "transvaluation of all values". Nearly all traditional values except courage—justice, charity, mercy, self-control, rational wisdom, even honesty, the willingness to conform to the truth—are declared vices that stand in the way of the Superman and his new morality, his "master morality". And traditional vices like cruelty, arbitrariness, egotism, aggression, and ruthlessness become virtues. The Nietzschean Superman becomes the new God by leaping over the confining walls of morality and religion, Socrates and Jesus. Nietzsche declared himself to be the Antichrist. (As far as I know, only one other writer ever made that claim in print: my colleague in the Boston College theology department, Mary Daly, who has described her life's work, her *summum bonum,* as "castrating God the Father". Jesuit schools have "come a long way, baby".)

There are strong elements of Nietzscheanism in Deconstructionism and also in radical feminism, both of which substitute power for goodness and truth. The line from *Macbeth* haunts me as prophetic when Lady Macbeth, becoming morally insane and demon-possessed, says to her dark gods, "unsex me here!"

Lewis says enough about Satan to fill a dozen dissertations, especially in *The Screwtape Letters, The Problem of Pain,* and *Mere Christianity.* He does not offer philosophical arguments against Satanism; that was Chamberlain's mistake. "This kind comes out only by prayer and fasting."

I think Nietzsche's "transvaluation of all values" is attractive to people mainly because of the prior appeal of his other heresy, that of the dullness of ("Apollonian") goodness and the beauty of ("Dionysian") badness. Satan has won many more souls through boredom than through cruelty.

Lewis' Historical Significance

The most horrible of all twenty heresies, Nietzschean Satanism, erupted into our century most spectacularly with the Nazis, who took Nietzsche as their guru. We cannot blame Nietzsche for the Nazis' racism, but we can surely blame him for their (and his) immorality, his exaltation of war, and his hatred of Jews and Christians. But Hitler was small potatoes; he was not even a thoroughgoing Nietzschean, much less the thoroughgoing Antichrist. He was only a preview of coming attractions, if we are to believe the prophecies in the New Testament.

The power of this heresy is still with us, however politically incorrect it has become. Its power can be seen in an unforgettable scene in that dreary, decadent, and brilliant movie *Cabaret.* Suddenly, in the middle of world-weary thirties' decadence, a band of idealistic "blond beasts", noble young Nazis, appear in an outdoor restaurant and stentorianly sing "Tomorrow Belongs to Me". Everyone is swept along and it becomes a sing-along, as the whole nation was soon to be. For nature abhors a vacuum, spiritual as well as physical. The vacuum of moral decadence is just as much with us here and now as it was there and then. As W. B. Yeats wrote, "The best lack all conviction, while the worst/ Are full of passionate intensity." We have not yet learned the obvious lesson from this bit of the past, and "those who do not learn from the past are condemned to repeat it." The next eruption of the demonic will probably appear much more civilized, like the Nazis' response to those who suspected the Holocaust: "What! Do you think we are *barbarians?*" Or like the line from *A Man for All Seasons:* "Come now, Thomas, this is England, not Spain!" This is America. We don't do holocausts here. (Tell that to the thirty million innocent babies already killed by our "healers'" scalpels, suction tubes, scalding salts, or skull-crushing pliers in their mothers' wombs.)

Moloch is never satisfied. He wants the blood of the old as well as the young. Ten years from now—maybe five—Dr. Kevorkian will be a folk hero. Once the camel's nose is under the tent, the rest of the camel will follow. It's a one-piece camel. Once a society or an individual denies the *Tao,* once Johnny can't tell right from wrong, once man plays God by creating values, all hell breaks loose.

To see how Lewis can help us in this apocalyptic time, let us briefly take stock of where we have come from in the last three or four centuries.

The grand strategy of modernism is the dethronement of religion. The first step was the (false) opposition between science and religion. This is the heart of rationalism and "modernism". The second stage, now called "post-modernism", is the (real) opposition of irrational desire to religion and also to science, especially the irrational desire of the ideological addiction to the sexual revolution. Some great Christian philosophers adopted rationalism and modernism—Descartes, Leibniz, Berkeley, Hegel—and in all cases it changed their Christianity rather than their Christianity changing it, as happened in the Middle Ages when Christianity changed and baptized Greek philosophy. Other great Christian philosophers adopted irrationalism against modernism—Pascal, Kierkegaard, Unamuno y Jugo—a leap over reason into the arms of God. This is always an option in any age, for those divine arms remain wide open; but it does not win philosophical battles; it leaves that battlefield.

Lewis still fights on the old battlefield of reason—not narrowed, scientialized modernist "reason", but old, big, deep, wide, broad, classical "reason". He is essentially an Augustinian, a Christian Platonist. (Remember the Professor in the Chronicles of Narnia: "It's all in Plato, all in Plato. What do they teach them in the schools nowadays?") *Miracles* fought against modernist, scientific rationalism, and *The Abolition of Man* combats postmodernist irrationalism.

Philosophy alone will not defeat our foe from Hell, of course, not even the best philosophy. Prayer, love, virtue, and sacrifice will. Ultimately, divine grace alone will. M-1s alone will not win the war; we need heavy artillery. Yet without the infantry, the tanks and artillery alone cannot win the war, either. Lewis' M-1 philosophical arguments, plus his and your and my prayers and works of charity, plus God's angel air force, will win. That is certain. Perhaps many corpses will be left strewn on the battlefield, perhaps the corpse of Western civilization will be there, but we will win, or God is a liar. Our fatherland is not America; it is the Kingdom of Heaven. We are travelers, just passing through this hotel. If the hotel does the scandalously simple thing—repents—it too will be saved; if not, not. No society has ever survived, or will ever survive, without morality; and no morality has ever survived without religion. There are only two roads, just as Psalm 1 so simply says. Or, as Lewis reminds us of our forgotten moral kindergarten, "Unless we return to the crude and nurserylike belief in objective values, we will surely perish."

If we do, it won't be his fault.

4

Can the Natural Law Ever Be Abolished from the Heart of Man?

Saint Thomas Aquinas assures us that the natural law can never be abolished from the heart of man (S. T. I–II, 94, 6). Is he right or is he wrong?

This is one of the few things absolutely necessary to think about today. I say "few" because in wartime, as in sickness, your focus and perspective narrow. You see that 90 percent of everything you habitually think or do is dispensable. You see most scholarship as "inchworm, inchworm, measuring the marigolds"; most social science as rearranging deck chairs on the *Titanic;* and most theologians as fiddlers on the roof, fiddling while Rome burns. (In a world without heroes, they play the part of Neros.)

Our question is a wartime question, in fact an apocalyptic question. Our question is whether there is a Brave New World at the end of our social mudslide. If anyone believes such language is exaggerated, I welcome him back from his nice vacation on another planet. For surely we are living through what may well turn out to be the most radical revolution in the history of human thought, a revolution which is not just a "culture war" but a spiritual war, a moral and religious war. This war has raged throughout this strangest of centuries. At the human heart of this war is the revolution in values, a revolution away from moral *laws* to moral "values", away from objective natural law to subjective human values. Our question here is: How far can this revolution go? The natural law has been battered and has lost many battles; will it finally lose the war? Aquinas says no. Is he right?

This revolution has won over the intelligentsia of Western civilization at a steadily increasing rate throughout this century, and it is percolating down to the masses through modern media faster than Christianity converted the world in the first few centuries. Dechristianization is happening faster than Christianization did. We are caught in the middle of a gigantic sea change, and in one sense it is more radical than the one two thousand years ago, for the same reason divorce is a more radical change than marriage and death more traumatic than birth.

The last two hundred years have seen a greater change than the previous two thousand—not just technologically but spiritually. To see this, just reflect that the spiritual differences between Virgil and Milton are not as great as those between Milton and Sartre; or that the differences between Homer and Shakespeare are not as great as those between Shakespeare and Bertrand Russell. To quote Chesterton again, the difference between those who worship one God and those who worship many is not as great as the difference between those who worship and those who do not.

The religious instinct and the moral instinct have not always been joined together as they are in Judaism, Christianity, and Islam, but they have always both characterized human nature throughout all of its known history on this planet and have been at least somewhat dependent on each other. Both instincts are innate, not derived from the empirical world. The fear (or awe or worship) of God is not derivable from the natural fear of tigers or lawyers, or even from the natural fear of suffering and dying. Similarly, the sense that I am obligated to help the needy or honor my promises is not deducible merely from the fact that the needy will suffer without me, or the fact that I may be caught and hurt if I do not honor my promises. The "ought" is a new dimension, not just more of the "is", as a cube is more than a square. Both religion and morality are givens, not derivations; innate instincts, not discoveries about the world; a priori, not a posteriori.

And both, in one century, are suddenly beginning to disappear, it seems.

Judaism, Christianity, and Islam all need morality as a prerequisite to religion, as Eastern or New Age religions do not. For without a real, objective morality, without a natural law, and without conscience, we have no natural knowledge of the character of this God, of our obligations to this God, and of our broken relationship with this God. The kind of God we might get to without a moral beginning is the God most Americans believe in, according to the polls. (Ninety percent of Americans believe in God, but only 13 percent believe in all Ten Commandments!) This is the Warm Fuzzy God, "The Force", either deistic or pantheistic, not a Person ("I Am") with a will and a law. So the abolition of the natural moral law would be like termites undermining the common foundation of all three Western religious buildings.

Few philosophers clearly see that this is no accident but deliberate strategy. The prophetic Italian Marxist Gramsci saw it and predicted that Marxist atheism would triumph not militarily or even politically but educationally, by infiltrating the intelligentsia. Get the teachers and you've got the students. This is exactly what is happening. The basic philosophical theses of Marxism are winning the world more solidly now, after its political collapse in 1989, than before. Just as Christianity did two thousand years earlier, it is winning minds and hearts rather than dictators and parliaments. Chesterton was one of the few who saw the direction of the danger. He said back in the twenties that "the real danger is not in Moscow but in Manhattan."

At the beginning of this century, only the outrageously avant-garde were atheists or moral subjectivists. Now as the century is ending, the three major mind-molding establishments in the Western world—formal education, entertainment (i.e., informal education), and journalism—are massively dominated by the subjectivists and secularists. There is manifold, abundant, incontrovertible statistical evidence both to define and prove this. (See, e.g., the poll of media personnel by Baltimore's Wirthlin Institute about five years ago.)

My question is: Will 2094 be to 1994 what 1994 is to 1894? If the present curve continues, will we reach a Brave New World, a new humanity, "men without chests"? Could it happen that the natural law will be abolished from the heart of man?

One is tempted to say no, because if so, then religion would also be abolished, and we know that the gates of Hell will not prevail against the Church. But we also know that there is coming a "Great Tribulation" so terrible that "if God had not shortened those days, no flesh would be saved." Please take a few minutes some time to let your thoughts sink into and swim around in that terrifying idea (or, rather, fact).

Let's try a thought experiment. What would you say if someone made the following serious, literal prediction? Within forty years, all public high schools in America will have sex clinics, à la Masters and Johnson—both heterosexual and homosexual. There will be state-sponsored sodomy lessons for teenagers. Sexual satisfaction will be enshrined as a constitutional right. Parental objections will be labelled "hate speech" and "fear-and-shame-based education" and made illegal. Drugs will be legal and available as cheaply and easily as ice cream. Suicide chambers will be provided. Dr. Kevorkian will be a folk hero. Euthanasia will also be a constitutional right, like abortion. The family will be redefined to include any voluntary sexual living arrangement, including group sex or sex with animals. Most children will be raised by the State and not know their own fathers. The Catholic Church, orthodox Judaism, and Islam will be denied civil rights because they alone will oppose this revolution. Most American Catholics will belong to "The American Catholic Church", which will break with Rome rather than with Washington. Catholics loyal to Rome will be persecuted for treason, like Roman Catholics in China. There will be increased violence throughout the nation, despite massive efforts to curb its symptoms, because it will be illegal to curb its sources, since that would be an establishment of religion.

Does this sound unbelievable? The changes during the last forty years are no less unbelievable. Suppose our ancestors in 1954 knew similar facts about 1994 (e.g., the 5000 percent rise in teen-age violence). They would find our world no less fantastic than we find this scenario. Why should the movement which has been gathering momentum for forty years slow down rather than speed up in the next forty?

Having thus established the practical relevance of my scholarly topic (in a rather unscholarly way), I will now introduce the players, or debaters, on the issue of *Summa* I–II, 94, 6: Can the natural law ever be abolished from the heart of man?

On the pro side, the side that maintains that it can, I call C. S. Lewis as my major witness and *The Abolition of Man* as my major text. Aiding him are Scott Peck, in *People of the Lie;* Walker Percy, in *The Thanatos Syndrome;* Aldous Huxley, in *Brave New World;* George Orwell, in *1984;* Alasdair MacIntyre, in *After Virtue;* and a few ragtag existentialists named Pascal, Nietzsche, Dostoyevsky, and Kierkegaard.

It sounds like a formidable team. Yet I have found that even more formidable thinkers, like Plato and even Aristotle, have a habit of losing debates with Aquinas. *I* certainly do. Every time I have differed with him, on every issue so far except one, he has eventually won me over and shown me the error of my ways, sometimes after many years, when I returned to the *Summa* to do some Summa-wrestling with this giant. (The only issue I still think he was wrong about is whether there are animals in Heaven. He says no. I think God let him goof there so we would not idolize him as infallible.)

Of course Aquinas is not the complete philosopher. No one is. There are neglected dimensions that need to be added, notably the personalistic, the "turn to the subject", that characterizes most modern Catholic philosophers, including the Church's current great philosopher-king. Like the natural law itself according to Aquinas (S. T. I–II, 94, 5), his philosophy is to be added to, but not subtracted from.

If Aquinas was wrong on whether the natural law can ever be abolished from the heart of man, it was a major error, and one which, if we succumbed to it, would give us a false sense of security in a desperate emergency—like not listening to the countdown of the nuclear clock. (Perhaps instead of the old "nuclear clock" we should have been watching the countdown to doomsday on the conscience clock, which has steadily been ticking away the deconstruction of conscience.)

Before calling on our debaters we must define our terms. In the question "whether the natural law can ever be abolished from the heart of man", there are six terms which may be misunderstood and thus need to be defined: (1) "law", (2) "natural", (3) "natural law", (4) "abolished", (5) "heart", and (6) "man".

1. By "law" I mean what Aquinas meant: an ordinance of reason for the common good, made by one in authority in a community and promulgated (S. T. I–II, 90, 4). The key term for our purposes in this definition is "reason". Law is rational, both in its origin and in its end. It is a product, not of power, but of insight and the will to order. And its end is the rationally understood benefit to the community of making men good (cf. S. T. I–II, 92, 1). Peter Maurin defined a good society as one that makes it easy to be good. That is the best definition of a good society that I know. Only a saint, a simpleton, or a child can answer a question that complex that simply.

The term "reason" has changed drastically since Aquinas.

Ever since Kant, it has meant something psychological and subjective (even if it is necessary and universal); something we do in our minds rather than something in nature. *Logos,* objective reason, has become an incomprehensible term; its holding place in the post-Kantian mind has shriveled up.

Ever since Descartes, "reason" has also meant primarily *ratio,* not *intellectus; dianoia,* not *epistēmē;* calculation, not understanding. This is why many otherwise sane professors seriously wonder whether computers think, or what difference there is between artificial intelligence and natural intelligence. Computers, like symbolic logic, do not begin with the first act of the mind. They don't understand anything at all, not even as much as an amoeba does.

Ultimately, the roots of the modern shrinking of reason go back to Ockham and Nominalism, the denial of objectively real essences to understand. We must free ourselves from the unholy trinity of shrinkers—first Ockham, then Descartes, then Kant—before we can understand what Aquinas means by "reason" and hence by "law".

2. By "natural" is meant "in accord with a thing's nature or essence". The category of the "natural" is another casualty of modern philosophy, humanism, secularism, technologism, scientism, subjectivism, and the other usual suspects. The notion that certain sexual acts are "unnatural" used to be a commonplace truism; now it is commonplace joke. One of the strongest pieces of evidence for the pro side in our debate about whether the natural law can be abolished from man's heart is modern man's radically new inability even to understand the meaning of the word "natural" when applied to human behavior. The most he can manage to mean here is often either (1) that the natural means the common, whatever most men in fact do, or (2) that the natural is what the ones who make the rules like and approve.

The notion of nature as essence and as principle of action has been largely lost—either denied or (worse) forgotten. Instead of "nature" meaning the essence of a thing ("first act" or "first actuality"), as the principle of its operation (which is "second act")—instead of meaning first act's great power or potency to issue forth in second act like a woman giving birth—the word now means to most minds simply the sum total of all the observed concrete entities in the universe: birds and bees and flowers and trees. It is not a power, or source of activity, but only the finished products. Thus "natural law" seems almost oxymoronic, since no law is ever observed as one of those concrete entities or finished products. The term "objective values" sounds equally oxymoronic to modern man, since he means by "values" something in our feelings and by "objective" something outside, like a rock.

3. By "natural law" is meant two things: first, that it is a law that is naturally *known,* innately known, instinctively known, known by natural reason; and second, that it is a law *based on* human nature and *for* the flourishing and fulfilling of human nature.

The notion of a natural law thus involves the notion of objective end and purpose. If all purposes and ends are only human and subjective, the idea of a natural law becomes groundless, for its ground is a human nature that has natural ends (e.g., procreation); and deliberately frustrating those ends (e.g., by contraception or sodomy) can then no longer be called "unnatural". This is already where most minds are today.

4. By "abolished" is meant not just temporarily forgotten but eradicated. We can temporarily forget anything at all, even our own existence, in moments of sleep or unconsciousness at one extreme or self-forgetful ecstasy at the other.

The pro side of this debate will maintain that it is possible to produce a race of "trousered apes"—men not just unwilling but unable to understand the natural law, not just for a moment but for a lifetime. They may understand social "appropriateness" and legal sanctions and the rules of the games people play (positive law), but they have lost the capacity, not only to believe, but even to understand the very concept of a natural moral law. Such, according to our pros, are increasingly many of our modernly educated children of the chimpanzees—the more modern, the more unnatural. For instance, studies have shown a distinct, direct link between level of education and willingness to inflict torture in the Nazi death camps. Today, there is a similar link between amount of education and willingness to murder unborn babies as well as old people who have lost their "quality of life".

5. By "heart" is meant not just feelings but mind; not just sentiment but consciousness; not just desire but understanding. "The heart has its *reasons*", said Pascal—one of the most abused quotations in history, almost always taken to justify exactly what it excludes: irrationality. It does not diminish reason; it extends it.

The heart is the organ by which we perceive and are moved by morality. We usually call it "conscience" (thus expanding the Thomistic meaning of the word a bit, including what he called "synderesis").

6. Finally, by "man" is meant the species, not the individual, or even all individuals. The very wording of our question assumes the falsity of Nominalism, assumes that there is such a thing as human nature. It then questions whether this nature can change at heart.

The doctrine of Original Sin implies that human nature did once radically change, at the Fall. In one sense, the pros in our debate contend that a greater change is happening today, for Adam had knowledge of the natural law both before and after the Fall. (Of course, in other ways, the present change is far less radical.)

A personal note, before the debate begins. This is a topic in which I am both interested and disinterested. Interested because I wonder whether my children and children's children will grow up on earth or in a Brave New World, and because as a member of this civilization I wonder whether the gates of Hell will prevail against her as they did against Sodom, Carthage, and the Third Reich. Disinterested because as of this writing, I do not think I know the answer, and I chose to write this essay to try to find out. I have no axe to grind, no thesis to defend.

We begin with the pro side. I will very briefly note evidence from a number of writers, in no close logical or chronological order, then give C. S. Lewis more time because I think *The Abolition of Man* the most formidable argument for the pro side.

Let us begin with Dr. Scott Peck. He is a good man. (I have met him, and was personally impressed.) He is also a man who believes in human goodness—a "liberal" in the old sense of being optimistic, idealistic, humanistic, and ethical. After writing one of the best-selling psychology books of the century, *The Road Less Travelled,* a book that celebrated the inner wisdom of the unconscious and the power of self-teaching and self-healing, Dr. Peck wrote a very different kind of book, *People of the Lie,* because to his extreme surprise he met what he had not believed existed before: living instances of genuinely amoral people, specimens that cannot exist according to the con side of our debate.

In these people the moral light had simply died. They lived Nietzsche's "most dangerous question", "Why truth? Why not rather untruth?" We stand aghast (or should) before the absolute audacity of this unanswerable question.

The question is unanswerable because all answering presupposes the value of truth. One who refuses truth cannot be refuted or healed with truth or its prophet, reason. There is in him no sense of *obligation,* even to truth, and therefore no obligation to anything. Meeting such a person feels like meeting a man without a head. And Scott Peck discovered that such people exist. If some exist now, more may exist soon and all may become such some day. So it is possible for the natural law to be abolished from the heart of man; there is experiential evidence for this.

The reason this is possible seems to be as follows. While it is impossible for us to create a natural law in a being that has none, as it is impossible to teach a stone to talk, it seems quite possible to destroy it in a being that had it, as it is possible to make a man dumb. Only God can create life, but man can destroy it. This seems to be true of spiritual life as well as physical life.

The next question is: How common are these "dead souls", as

Gogol called them, these spiritual corpses? Are they rare, as Peck thinks? Or are they common? There is reason to think they are becoming very common indeed. Alasdair MacIntyre, in *After Virtue,* contends that the moral language that we (i.e., both we philosophers and we ordinary men) still use today masks its own meaninglessness; that it is a dead relic of a living moral language, the linguistic rubble left from a catastrophe that we have not noticed because the words, like the façades of large buildings, have remained even after the buildings have been gutted and are largely uninhabited. He writes: "What we possess, if this view is true, are those fragments of a conceptual scheme, parts, which now lack those contexts from which their significance derived. We possess indeed simulacra of morality, we continue to use many of the key expressions. But we have—very largely, if not entirely— lost our comprehension, both theoretical and practical, of morality" (p. 2). The best that MacIntyre himself has been able to come up with in reply, despite his conversion to Catholicism, is what seems to be largely Cultural Relativism in a new suit, in *Whose Justice? Whose Morality?*

MacIntyre has not *proved* his pessimistic contention in *After Virtue.* But he has shown that one of the main arguments for the con position (Aquinas' position) is fallacious: the argument that we still argue morally, that moral discourse is even more popular today than ever. This premise does not entail the conclusion that morality remains. Maybe we're talking so much about it not because it's living but precisely because it's dying. Morality may be in the same boat as sex: the market is glutted with books because the pipes are broken and the house is flooded and the plumbers can't fix it. How-to-fix-it books appear only when something has stopped working, not when it is working. And sex is certainly not working. The two most easily documentable changes since the sexual revolution are: (1) people are having much, much more sex, and more kinds, than ever before in history, and (2) they are more worried and angry and unhappy about it than ever before in history. Moral discourse seems to be suffering the same fate: increased quantity substituting for diminishing quality.

Walker Percy has said much the same thing about language. So did Hemingway in *A Farewell to Arms* when he had his hero say that the only meaningful and noble words in war are names— concrete human beings and places where they died. All the abstract words, all the reasons, explanations, causes, values, and ideologies, had become a travesty. And, of course, the classic fictional example of the deconstruction of meaningful language is Newspeak in Orwell's *1984,* and the slogans in *Animal Farm.* Many observers of the social scene have noted the increasing resemblance of ordinary language to bureaucratic language and of bureaucratic language to Newspeak. Once there are no linguistic holding-places for moral concepts, the concepts, homeless, will die. That is why one of the basic planks in Confucius' platform for social reform was "the restoration of [proper] names". Alas, no Confucius looms on our horizon.

The New Man that seems to be emerging is not immoral but amoral. He is not the serial killer—they have always been around— but the killer of conscience. Now there seem to be two different ways for old Screwtape to try to kill conscience, God's inner prophet: consciously or unconsciously. The conscious attempt, by fictional figures like Raskalnikov in Dostoyevsky's *Crime and Punishment* and Ivan Karamazov in *The Brothers Karamazov* and by real philosophers like Nietzsche, does not work. All three believed the same thing: if there is no God, everything is permissible; slave morality does not bind masters, sheep morality does not apply to wolves, man's morality will not hold back Overman. But all three were eventually tormented by guilt and/or insanity. They were only temporarily successful in killing conscience; it rose from the dead and took its revenge like a ghost.

Much more successful, from the viewpoint of Satanic strategy, is the unconscious way, the slow, insidious drip that blurs the point of the icicle of conscience until it is all melted into a warm pool of pop psychobabble. Not Raskalnikov but Camus' Meursault is the New Man. *The Stranger* is more terrifying than the Godfather. He is simply indifferent. Though Meursault is fictional, he was conceived by a real mind on the basis of real experience of real men, and he arrested the attention of millions of real readers who accepted him as real based on their real experience of real men. No fiction, not even fantasy, can be successful without telling the truth. There are Meursaults. And they are not all in prison. Some even manifest the one and only passion Meursault manifested at the end, the passion against the priest, against Christianity, against morality and religion, against the natural law. Surely mushy theists must envy moral theists as geldings envy stallions.

Here is Pascal's description of the geldings, in a prophetic passage from the *Pensées*. It describes the man indifferent even to the most powerful wakeup call God ever used, death:

> It is . . . quite certainly a great evil to have such doubts [about God and immortality], but . . . the doubter who does not seek is at the same time very unhappy and very wrong. If in addition he feels a calm satisfaction, which he openly professes . . . I can find no terms to describe so extravagant a creature. . . . How can such an argument as this occur to a reasonable man?
>
> I do not know who put me into the world, nor what the world is, nor what I am myself. . . . I see the terrifying spaces of the universe hemming me in, and I find myself attached to one corner of this vast expanse without knowing why I have been put in this place rather than that, or why the brief span of life allotted to me should be assigned to one moment rather than another of all the eternity which went before me and all that which will come after me. . . . All I know is that I must soon die, but what I know least about is this very death which I cannot evade.
>
> Just as I do not know whence I came, so I do not know whither I am going. All I know is that when I leave this world I shall fall forever into nothingness, or into the hands of an angry God; but I do not know which of these two states is to be my

eternal lot. Such is my state, full of weakness and uncertainty. And my conclusion from all this is that I must pass my days without a thought of seeking what is to happen to me. Perhaps I might find some enlightenment in my doubts, but I do not want to take the trouble ... and afterwards, as I sneer at those who are striving to this end ... I will go without fear or foresight to face so momentous an event, and allow myself to be carried off limply to my death, uncertain of my future state for all eternity.

This is observation. Such men exist. What follows is evaluation, Pascal's commentary on these New Men:

The fact that there exist men who are indifferent to the loss of their being and the peril of an eternity of wretchedness is against nature. With everything else they are quite different: they fear the most trifling things, foresee and feel them; and the same man who spends so many days and nights in fury and despair at losing some office or at some imaginary affront ... is the very one who knows that he is going to lose everything through death but feels neither anxiety nor emotion. It is a monstrous thing to see one and the same heart at once so sensitive to minor things and so strangely insensitive to the greatest. It is an incomprehensible spell, a supernatural torpor that points to a supernatural power as its cause.

Eighty-two percent of Americans believe Hell exists. Only 4 percent fear that they will go there.

Here is another statistic, from another field, which illustrates the same principle. Among fifty industrialized nations, American high school students scored the lowest in the world in math. But they scored the highest in the world in self-esteem, in how well they *thought* they had done in math. There are more connections than most people think between math and morality.

Many other thinkers have prophesied the emergence of the New Man—e.g., David Riesman (and Nathan Glazer) in *The Lonely Crowd*: the New Man who is neither "tradition-directed" nor "inner-directed" but "other-directed", the man with no source of morality but common feeling, consensus, fashion, and peer pressure.

We could mention other prophets: Ortega y Gasset, Oswald Spengler, T. S. Eliot—but the prophetic palm must go to Nietzsche, who prophesied the emergence of not one but two New Men. One is "the Last Man", the blinking conformist whom Nietzsche despises, just as the other prophets do. But the second is the Overman, who kills God and conscience, religion and morality, to become the new god himself. "The Last Man" is passionless; the Overman passionate. Both are godless, but "the Last Man" is Meursault, the Overman is Raskalnikov. "The Last Man" seeks peace at any price; the Overman seeks war at any cost. An imperfect preview of "the Last Man" was Chamberlain; an imperfect preview of the Overman was Hitler.

One need not share Nietzsche's atheism to agree with his historical, not theological, dictum that "God is dead"—i.e., that faith in God is dead as a functional center for Western civilization, that we are now a planet detached from its sun. One need not share Nietzsche's refusal of morality and natural law to agree with his observation that Western man is increasingly denying morality and natural law; that we are well on our way to the Brave New World.

The "pro" side of our debate now calls as its witness Nietzsche's opposite—as passionate and brilliant a Christian as Nietzsche was an atheist, namely, Søren Kierkegaard—to my mind the greatest Protestant thinker of all time. The unifying thread through his whole astonishingly kaleidoscopic authorship is the three "stages" ("aesthetic", "ethical", and "religious"). These are designed to dispel the three fundamental illusions that block modern man from reaching the end of life on earth and the single point of all Kierkegaard's writings, "becoming a Christian". First, there is the illusion of thinking you are living in religious categories when you are only living in ethical ones. Second, there is the illusion of thinking you are living in ethical categories when you are only living in aesthetic, hedonistic ones. Third, there are the passionless nothings who do not even rise to the aesthetic.

Both the passionate aesthete and the passionless pre-aesthete lack an awareness of the natural moral law. The infant is the perfect aesthete; he is born living the philosophy of "I want what I want when I want it." Some men are only large, sophisticated infants who have substituted sophisticated pleasures for unsophisticated ones, e.g., science or scholarship for the bottle, or philanthropy for bullying. "Whatever turns you on."

The pre-aesthete is even more amoral. He is Pascal's "indifferent" man (Kierkegaard was deeply indebted to Pascal). Even the aesthete detests him, and says (in *Either/Or*):

> Let others complain that the age is wicked; my complaint is that it is wretched, for it lacks passion. Men's thoughts are thin and flimsy like lace; they are themselves pitiable like the lacemakers. The thoughts of their hearts are too paltry to be sinful. For a worm it might be regarded as a sin to harbor such thoughts, but not for a being made in the image of God.... Out upon them! This is the reason my soul always turns back to the Old Testament and to Shakespeare. I feel that those who speak there are at least human beings: they hate, they love, they murder their enemies and curse their descendents throughout all generations, they sin.
>
> So many live on in a quiet state of perdition ... they live their lives, as it were, outside of themselves, they vanish like shadows, their immortal soul is blown away, and they are not alarmed by the problem of its immortality, for they are already in a state of dissolution before they die.

The "indifferent" man is even farther from morality, and therefore from the true religion of which morality is the foundation, than is the aesthete or passionate atheist and rebel. As George Macdonald says, revolt against God is far closer to faith than indifference to him. For (as Rollo May says), the opposite of love is not hate but indifference.

The New Man and the modern world are full of this opposite

of love. Such a world talks endlessly about "love", the word substituting for the reality. Its philosophy can be summarized in a single syllogism. It identifies the good with love and love with sex, thus the good with sex. It's the only thing that overcomes indifference. (I have a good, pious, wise professor friend who is tempted to publish a satirical article entitled "Sex As the Only Absolute Good", but fears that both his fellow professors and his students would not take it satirically but propagandize it as a manifesto.)

I think the main reason a Brave New World is attractive, both to its own fictional inhabitants and to people in the real world, is that it is apparently a world full of love. The first time I taught the book was the occasion for a profound shock. I discovered the New Men: my students. (This was back in the sixties.) In discussing the book in class, it gradually dawned on me that many of my students were fundamentally misunderstanding it as a utopia instead of a dystopia, thinking Huxley was advocating it. Then came the second, deeper shock: they were all for it! They longed to live in Huxley's Brave New World. After all, in that world "everybody's happy now." For there's free sex ("pneumatic"!) with no social sanctions and no guilt; free drugs ("soma"); and endless mindless entertainment ("centrifugal bumble-puppy"), but no pain, no passion, no agony, no ecstasy, no drama, no Shakespeare, no Michelangelo, no Beethoven—in other words, life as it actually exists for the average American teenager today.

What we want, we get. The ancient image of the wishing tree in the Hindu scriptures is accurate—from a Christian point of view, too: Heaven and Hell are both freely chosen. What we most deeply want, we get. All who seek, find. And today we seek a Brave New World. Therefore today we are getting there. In *Brave New World Revisited,* written a generation later, Huxley said he was wrong about only one of his predictions: the timing. It is coming much faster than he thought.

If a time machine could dip into the fifties and pluck out an uncle, an ordinary uncle, deposit him in the nineties, and simply show him the empirical facts—MTV, Howard Stern, public high school sex education classes—he would probably literally be unable to believe it. Many people today do not believe it: they simply do not know what is happening. According to one poll, one-third of Americans do not believe the Holocaust ever happened. Nearly nine-tenths of Americans do not know that over a million and a half mothers kill their unborn babies every year.

The Brave New World countdown clock continues. Just recently, a federal judge ruled that a male boss' hand on a female employee's shoulder constituted sexual harassment but that there was no such thing as any reasonable definition of "obscenity". Not long ago the State of Massachusetts funded, with public tax money, a conference organized by Planned Parenthood that put into the hands of all public school personnel who came material that now labels any sex education that advocates abstinence, whether exclusively or not, "fear-and-shame-based sex education". It also listed the names of "the opposition", including all conservative columnists, talk-show hosts, and organizations like Focus on the Family, that criticized abortion or unrestricted sex. Topping the list of these new McCarthyites, of course, was the Catholic Church.

When two local liberal Jewish writers protested my local neighborhood high school sponsoring a sex education drama in which a nun was raped and pleaded for more, the local media labeled and linked them with "the Christian Fundamentalist far Right". The media can now get away with this knee-jerk nonsense because education has been so severely dumbed down that people won't or can't think. (By the way, Jews and Muslims are now virtually the only ones who protest anti-Catholic bigotry. Most Catholics are too wimpy.)

Human embryos have now been cloned (though not yet kept alive). The genome project—total genetic mapping—is only a few years away. So is the human body shop. Subliminal perception, sleep-teaching, hypnotherapy, and other irresistible applied psychological techniques have long been in place, like nuclear arsenals, only waiting for the will to use them. Traditional morality remains to dam this flood, but the dam is wearing thinner every year.

The hard totalitarianism of *1984* is unlikely, that is, external political and military totalitarianism. Hitler blew the cover on that scheme from Hell, Plan A. But Plan B, the soft totalitarianism of a Brave New World, free, popular, and very scientific, is panting at the door.

If we truly and passionately despise all totalitarianism, why is it so popular? We get the society we create, and we create the society we want. It is not imposed on us by the gods.

American journalists who visited Hitler's Germany in the thirties were scandalized not only by Hitler's power but by his popularity. Most Germans loved him—fanatically. These Americans had never read or understood Dostoyevsky's "Grand Inquisitor" or the power that drives us to rid ourselves of our nagging consciences and of the agonizing burden of freedom, even if the way to do that is to give them into the hands of a dictator. Dictators do not come into the human race from without, from Mars. They erupt from within, like hemorrhoids, from an infected body, from the one fact no secularist ever dares to face: Original Sin.

I now conclude my case for the pro side of the debate with C. S. Lewis. I shall concentrate on *The Abolition of Man,* but I first quote a passage from "The Poison of Subjectivism" about the apocalyptic consequences of denying the natural law. *The Abolition of Man* then explores the even more radical consequences of the even more radical step of abolishing not just belief in it but awareness of it.

> Until modern times no thinker of the first rank ever doubted that our judgements of value were rational judgements or that what they discovered was objective. . . . The modern view is very different. It does not believe that value judgements are really judgements at all. They are sentiments, or complexes, or attitudes, produced in a community by the pressure of its

environment and its traditions, and differing from one community to another. To say that a thing is good is merely to express our feeling about it; and our feeling about it is the feeling we have been socially conditioned to have.

But if this is so, then we might have been conditioned to feel otherwise. 'Perhaps,' thinks the reformer or the educational expert, 'it would be better if we were. Let us improve our morality.' Out of this apparently innocent idea comes the disease that will certainly end our species (and, in my view, damn our souls) if it is not crushed: the fatal superstition that men can create values. . . .

Many a popular planner on a democratic platform, many a mild-eyed scientist in a democratic laboratory means, in the last resort, just what the Fascist means. He believes that 'good' means whatever men are conditioned to approve. He believes that it is the function of him and his kind to condition men; to create consciences by eugenics, psychological manipulation of infants, state education, and mass propaganda. Because he is confused, he does not fully realize that those who create conscience cannot be subject to conscience themselves. But he must awake to the logic of his position sooner or later; and when he does, what barrier remains between us and the final division of the race into a few Conditioners who stand themselves outside morality and the many conditioned in whom such morality as the experts choose is produced at the experts' pleasure? . . . The very idea of freedom presupposes some objective moral law which overarches rulers and ruled alike. Subjectivism about values is eternally incompatible with democracy. We and our rulers are of one kind only so long as we are subject to one law. But if there is no Law of Nature, the ethos of any society is the creation of its rulers, educators, and Conditioners; and every creator stands above and outside his own creation.

The apocalyptic practical consequences of this theoretical Subjectivism, the denial of the natural law, are shown in *The Abolition of Man,* surely one of the most prophetic books of modern times. Part 1, "Men without Chests", points out that our educational systems are already producing the New Men, the "men without chests", men without operative organs of apprehending objective values, or the natural law, or the *Tao.* This man is "the mere trousered ape who has never been able to conceive of the Atlantic as anything more than so many million tons of cold salt water".

Many others have bemoaned this change, but Lewis sees the radical nature of it better than most of his contemporaries do because of his deeper and longer historical sense: "Until quite modern times all teachers and even all men believed the universe to be such that certain emotional reactions on our part could be either congruous or incongruous to it—believed, in fact, that objects did not merely receive, but could *merit,* our approval or disapproval, our reverence or our contempt."

Add "volitional" to "emotional" and you have here the concept of the natural law, which Lewis defines as follows: "It is the doctrine of objective value, the belief that certain attitudes are really true, and others really false, to the kind of thing the universe is and the kind of things we are."

Lewis calls the spiritual organ in us by which we apprehend the *Tao* "the chest". It is what Scripture calls the "heart". It seems to include both a cognitive and an affective dimension: awareness of moral obligation and feeling obliged by it. Lewis emphasizes the affective dimension of it in saying it distinguishes us both from angels and animals, pure spirits and pure organisms. A Thomist would emphasize instead the volitional component and see it as something common to men and angels. But that correction does not affect Lewis' argument, I think.

Lewis says that "the operation of *The Green Book* [the typical school textbook Lewis uses as a case in point] and its kind is to produce what may be called men without chests"; and "the practical result of education in the spirit of *The Green Book* must be the destruction of the society which accepts it." (Notice the prophetic tone: "must be", not "may be". Certain doom lies along this path, though it is not certain that we will continue along this path. All prophets include a note of doom and a note of free choice.)

After part 2 defines and defends the *Tao*, part 3 widens our focus by asking the question: Into what kind of society is this new education now being inserted? What is the social context of the new moral Subjectivism? The answer is: a society with a new *summum bonum:* applied science, or technology, or "Man's conquest of Nature".

The program of this new end and purpose to human life is not just a gradual steady incline; a critical turning point lies in the road, and we are today accelerating to that critical point. Here is Lewis' analysis of that point. I beg your leave for an unusually long quotation because the issue is crucial, and Lewis' analysis is clearer and more compelling than any other I have ever seen:

> In order to understand fully what Man's power over Nature, and therefore the power of some men over other men, really means, we must picture the race extended in time from the date of its emergence to that of its extinction. Each generation exercises power over its successors: and each, in so far as it modifies the environment bequeathed to it [by technology] and rebels against tradition [especially by moral Subjectivism], resists and limits the power of its predecessors. This modifies the picture which is sometimes painted of a progressive emancipation from tradition and a progressive control of natural processes resulting in a continual increase of human power. In reality, of course, if any one age [ours? the twenty-first century?] really attains, by eugenics and scientific education, the power to make its descendants what it pleases, all men who live after it are the patients of that power. They are weaker, not stronger; for though we may have put wonderful machines in their hands we have pre-ordained how they are to use them. And if, as is almost certain, the age which had thus attained maximum power over posterity were also the age most emancipated from tradition, it would be engaged in reducing the power of its predecessors almost as drastically as that of its successors. . . . The real picture is that of one dominant age . . . which resists all previous ages most successfully and dominates all subsequent ages most irresistibly, and thus is the real master of the human species. But even within this master generation (itself an infini-

tesimal minority of the species) the power will be exercised by a minority smaller still. Man's conquest of Nature, if the dreams of some scientific planners are realized, means the rule of a few hundreds of men over billions upon billions of men. . . .

The final stage is come when Man by eugenics, by pre-natal conditioning, and by an education and propaganda based on a perfect applied psychology, has obtained full control over himself. *Human* nature will be the last part of Nature to surrender to Man. . . .

But the situation to which we must look forward will be novel in two respects. In the first place, the power will be enormously increased. . . . The second difference is even more important. In the older systems both the kind of man the teachers wished to produce and their motives for producing him were prescribed by the *Tao* — a norm to which the teachers themselves were subject and from which they claimed no liberty to depart. They did not cut men to some pattern they had chosen. They handed on what they had received; they initiated the young neophyte into the mystery of humanity which overarched him and them alike. It was but old birds teaching young birds to fly. This will be changed. Values are now mere natural phenomena. Judgements of value are to be produced in the pupil as part of the conditioning. Whatever *Tao* there is will be the product, not the motive, of education.

. . . Simple-minded critics may ask 'Why should you suppose they [the Conditioners] will be such bad men?' But I am not supposing them to be bad men. They are, rather, not men (in the old sense) at all. . . . Stepping outside the *Tao*, they have stepped into the void. Nor are their subjects necessarily unhappy men. [Remember *Brave New World!*] They are not men at all: they are artifacts. Man's final conquest has proved to be the abolition of Man.

. . . I am very doubtful whether history shows us one example of a man who, having stepped outside traditional morality and attained power, has used that power benevolently. I am inclined to think that the Conditioners will hate the conditioned. Though regarding as an illusion the artificial conscience which they produce in us their subjects, they will yet perceive that it creates in us an illusion of meaning for our lives which compares favourably with the futility of their own: and they will envy us as eunuchs envy men [or as Hollywood moviemakers envy the Bible Belters they trash].

The picture is more terrifying than nuclear war to one who values souls more than bodies. Our question here is not that of forecasting whether we will actually create this Brave New World. Nor is that Lewis' question. His question is rather that of the prophets. It is not foretelling so much as forthtelling. It is the publication of the road map and the demand that we ask ourselves: *Quo vadis?* Where does this road lead? It is up to the traveler, both individually and collectively, to choose to turn back or not, to repent or to apostasize, to be regressive or progressive down the mudslide to Hell.

Our question here is neither of these two: neither whether the road is leading to Hell's victory of a Brave New World (I think it is clear that it is) nor whether we will get off the slide before we hit bottom (no one knows that but God); but whether it is *possible,* whether "men without chests" can exist, whether Aquinas is wrong when he says the natural law cannot be abolished from the heart of man.

Lewis pretty clearly thinks it *is* possible: "It is in Man's power to treat himself as a mere 'natural object' and his own judgements of value as raw material for scientific manipulation to alter at will."

The only dam to this flood is the *Tao:* "Only the *Tao* provides a common human law of action which can over-arch both rulers and ruled alike. A dogmatic belief in objective values is necessary to the very idea of a rule which is not tyranny or an obedience which is not slavery."

This may seem extreme, but there can be no third, mediating possibility: the logic of the situation makes a comfortable humanism impossible. For

either we are rational spirit obliged for ever to obey the absolute values of the *Tao,* or else we are mere nature to be kneaded and cut into new shapes for the pleasures of masters who must, by hypothesis, have no motive but their own 'natural' impulses. ...Nature, untrammelled by values, rules the Conditioners and, through them, all humanity. Man's conquest of Nature turns out, in the moment of its consummation, to be Nature's conquest of Man.

This is the war we are in the midst of right now. As I write, I read a column by Joseph Sobran which reports that

the Clinton administration has just approved a grant of $4.5 million for fetal tissue research, which involves using the brain matter from slaughtered fetuses in the brains of Parkinson's patients. And this is the season when we are being reminded of how terrible the Nazis were.

This may be only the beginning. It appears that slaughtered children may soon become mothers. British doctors have succeeded in taking ova from animal fetuses, fertilizing them, and implanting them in other animals, which in due course give birth to them. The docs expect to be able to do this with human fetuses within three years. Imagine learning that your actual mother had been aborted. . . .

Such is the world the Clintons are helping usher us into. . . . Their agenda, which they themselves may not fully comprehend, is what C. S. Lewis called "the abolition of man"—the denial, not only in theory but in practice, of the human essence, of natural law. His little book by that title becomes more prophetic every year. It was written during World War II but looked far beyond the War, warning his readers that the British themselves included people who subscribed to philosophies as dehumanizing as Nazism. What he sensed, we see with our own eyes.

Our public educational establishment is even more committed to "Green Books" and is even more powerful than in Lewis' day, not only in classrooms but in movie theaters and newsrooms as well. We are big in the tummy with a new world, the world Lewis described as "the world of post-humanity, which, some knowingly and some unknowingly, nearly all are at present labouring to produce". Let us pray and work for the abortion of this pregnancy, for it is the Devil's child we carry in our womb.

Now let us hear Aquinas.

I am reluctant to set two of my very favorite writers of all time against each other. But the issue is too important for personal attachments to intrude; we must all say, like Aristotle, "dear indeed is Plato, but dearer still the truth." Of course Aquinas would agree with Lewis' principles, with the *Tao,* and with his jeremiad against the terrible consequences of denying it. The only thing he would disagree with, I think, is the possibility of the "abolition of man". Things can certainly get very, very bad, he would say—he was no naïve optimist or humanist, he read his Bible—but not that bad. Abolish the natural law from the heart of man and you have abolished human nature, yes. But it (and thus man) cannot be abolished.

The single short article that addresses that point can be found in S. T. I–II, 94, 6, with important preliminaries in the previous five articles. Aquinas' case can be summarized in seven points, seven reasons for the negative answer. Though Aquinas does not offer a single syllogistic argument whose conclusion is the thesis of the article, that the natural law can never be abolished from the heart of man, and in that sense he does not prove his conclusion at all (a rather unusual state of affairs for a *Summa* article!), there are seven implicit arguments to be found here.

First, article 1 of the same Question had asked "Whether the natural law is a habit?" If it is, then even if it were forgotten and not used, it would remain. Stones habitually fall, and when the hand that arrests their fall is withdrawn, they revert to their natural habit. So if the natural law were habitual, it would be ineradicable. Now Aquinas says that the natural law is itself not a habit, but that the precepts of it remain in the reason habitually even when forgotten. So in effect it is a habit. Here is the passage: "The precepts of the natural law are sometimes considered by reason actually, while sometimes they are in the reason only habitually; in this way the natural law may be called a habit." A habit remains even when unused, for "sometimes a man is unable to make use of that which is in him habitually on account of some impediment; thus, on account of sleep, a man is unable to use the habit of science. In like manner, through the deficiency of his age, a child cannot use the habit of understanding of principles, or the natural law, which is in him habitually."

However, Aquinas here only *distinguishes* between habitual and actual; he does not *prove* here that the natural law is in us habitually and is therefore ineradicable. If it is habitual, it is ineradicable. But why is it habitual? Article 2 supplies the answer to this Question: because it is self-evident. And here is the second point in our seven-point argument.

Aquinas says in article 2 that

> the precepts of the natural law are to the practical reason what the first principles of demonstrations are to the speculative reason [Lewis says exactly the same thing in *The Abolition of Man;* he calls these precepts 'axioms'] because both are self-evident first principles. . . . But some propositions are self-evident only to the wise, who understand the meaning of the terms of such propositions: thus to one who understands that an angel is not a body, it is self-evident that an angel is not circumscriptively in a place; but this is not self-evident to the unlearned, for they cannot grasp it. . . . Now as *being* is the first thing that falls under the apprehension simply, so *good* is the first thing that falls under the apprehension of the practical reason, which is directed to action: since every agent acts for an end under the aspect of good. Consequently the first principle in the practical reason is one founded on the notion of good, viz. that *good is that which all things seek after.* Hence this is the first precept of law, that *good is to be done and pursued, and evil is to be avoided.* All other precepts of the natural law are based on this; so that whatever the practical reason naturally apprehends as man's good (or evil) belongs to the precepts of the natural law as something to be done or avoided.
>
> [Now] all those things to which man has a natural inclination

are naturally apprehended by reason as being good. In man there is first of all an inclination to good in accordance with the nature which he has in common with all substances; inasmuch as every substance seeks the preservation of its own being, according to its nature; and by reason of this inclination, whatever is a means of preserving human life and of warding off its obstacles, belongs to the natural law.

Secondly, there is in man an inclination to things that pertain to him more specially, according to that nature which he has in common with other animals: and in virtue of this inclination, those things are said to belong to the natural law 'which nature has taught to all animals,' such as sexual intercourse, education of offspring, and so forth.

Thirdly, there is in man an inclination to good according to the nature of his reason, which nature is proper to him: thus man has a natural inclination to know the truth about God [!], and to live in society: and in this respect, whatever pertains to this inclination belongs to the natural law, for instance, to avoid ignorance.

This gives us a third reason for believing that the natural law is ineradicable: not only is it cognitively self-evident (reason no. 2) but it is also a natural inclination (reason no. 3).

A fourth reason is implied in article 3 of the same Question: "All acts of virtue are prescribed by the natural law." Thus, without the natural law, there is no virtue at all. If that situation is impossible, then man minus natural law is equally impossible.

A fifth reason, in article 4, is that the natural law is "the same in all men". Now what is always found the same in any being is either its genus, or its specific difference, or a necessary property that flows from either the genus or the specific difference or both, and thus is equally ineradicable. You can't change a species. But "the trousered ape" or the "men without chests" would be a change in species—in necessary property, at least. It would be neither man nor ape—an ape with an intellect but no conscience. That is an oxymoron (or an apeamoron).

To accommodate the empirical facts of important moral diversity here, Aquinas makes a reasonable distinction:

> The natural law, as to general principles, is the same for all, both as to rectitude [what is objectively right] and as to knowledge [what man knows to be right]. But as to certain matters of detail, which are conclusions, as it were, of those general principles, it is the same for all in the majority of cases, both as to rectitude and as to knowledge, and yet in some few cases it may fail, both as to rectitude, by reason of certain obstacles . . . and as to knowledge, since in some the reason is perverted by passion, or evil habit . . . thus formerly theft, although it is expressly contrary to the natural law, was not considered wrong among the Germans, as Julius Caesar relates.

San Francisco does not refute Aquinas. He was not ignorant of ensconced perversions. But even these do not simply abolish the natural law.

A sixth reason, in article 5, is that the natural law cannot be changed by subtraction, only by addition (since many things for the benefit of human life are added as history moves on). Abolition of the natural law itself would be the supreme, complete example of change by subtraction.

However, in each of these "arguments" so far, all we have is Aquinas supplying a premise which is just as controversial as the conclusion. From each premise it follows, indeed, that the natural law cannot be abolished; but the other side would deny each premise. We have not yet met the enemy and made him ours.

A seventh reason comes closer, in article 6. It consists in the fact that all three objections to the thesis (that the natural law is ineradicable) are adequately refuted by making reasonable distinctions.

The first objection is that sin blots out the law of righteousness, or law of nature, according to a gloss on Romans 2:14. The reply is that "sin blots out the law of nature in particular cases, not universally except perchance in regard to the secondary precepts." However, this is only stated, defined, distinguished, not proved.

The second objection is that "the law of grace is more efficacious than the law of nature. But the law of grace is blotted out by sin. Much more, therefore, can the law of nature be blotted out." The reply is that "although grace is more efficacious than nature, yet nature is more essential to man, and therefore more enduring."

And the third objection is that "many things are enacted by men which are contrary to the law of nature." The reply is that this is true only of the "secondary precepts".

The crucial question here is whether the Ten Commandments (specifically, for our culture, the sixth) are part of the primary or secondary precepts. If primary, they cannot be blotted out. Secondary precepts then would be restricted to applications of them (e.g., Pay your taxes as an application of Thou shalt not steal; and Do not sodomize as an application of Do not commit adultery). If they are secondary, however, they can be blotted out, and all we are left with for the primary precepts would be the abstract, Kantianly-formal "Do good and avoid evil." Aquinas does not mean this. For he speaks of the primary precepts in the plural, not simply "precept" in the singular.

But when we look to the body of article 6 for a crucial proof of the thesis that the natural law cannot be abolished from the heart of man, we are disappointed to find only an *explanation,* in the form of two *distinctions,* but not a *demonstration.* These distinctions, however, are important enough to admit and explain the data about human wickedness and blindness that constitutes much of the evidence for the other side, the pro side, of our debate. Thus Aquinas does declaw some more of his (pessimistic) opponents' objections here. This is what he says:

> There belong to the natural law, first, certain most general precepts, that are known to all; and secondly, certain secondary and more detailed precepts, which are, as it were, conclusions following closely from first principles. As to those general principles, the natural law, in the abstract, can no wise be blotted out from men's hearts. But it is blotted out in the case of

a particular action in so far as reason is hindered from applying the general principle to a particular point of practice on account of concupiscence or some other passion. But as to the other, i.e., the secondary precepts, the natural law can be blotted out from the human heart, either by evil persuasions [the Green Book!], just as in speculative matters errors occur [even] in respect to necessary conclusions; or by vicious customs [MTV?] and corrupt habits [condoms?], as among some men, theft, and even [!] unnatural vices, as the Apostle states (Romans 1), were not esteemed sinful.

Note, by the way, that the Roman world the Apostle described was even more corrupt than ours in practice. But this should not temper our pessimism. Consider the following dilemma. One wonders whether the average upper-middle class Roman citizen who took a moral holiday in Corinth really believed that moral values were subjective and relative, or knew better and was nagged by conscience. If he killed his conscience, so can we; if he did not, even this conscience-filled world was so wicked that God had to come to die to save it, and if we revert to its wickedness while refusing its Savior, is our future any brighter than that of pagan Rome?

Why did Aquinas not supply any direct demonstration of his thesis in the crucial article (6)? The con side (who agree with him) would say that he considered it self-evident, or nearly so. The pro side (the pessimists, who disagree with him) would say that he could not. What follows is a feeble attempt to complete Aquinas' argument by adding six reasons for his thesis. Whether they are demonstrative or only probable is a further question. The reasons are, in summary:

1. an a posteriori argument from past history: that history shows no comparably apocalyptic change;

2. an a posteriori argument from observation of the present: that most people retain a knowledge of the natural law even when programmed to deny it;

3. an a posteriori argument from the present about the likely future: that the counter-force of ordinary people is even now rising against the relativistic "experts" or "Conditioners";

4. an a priori argument about the human essence: that no creature can change its species or essence, and the natural law is indispensable to the human essence;

5. an a fortiori argument from demon possession: that if moral sanity can be restored even to the demon-possessed, it can also be restored to those possessed by relativism;

6. an argument from divine revelation: that God will always trump sin with grace and not allow his image to be obliterated.

First, the empirical argument from the past. History bears witness to Aquinas' contention. For no matter how wicked and foolish a society gets — and there have been spectacular examples — mankind is always pulled back to a knowledge of the natural law, though often at the expense of the temporal death of the offending society and the eternal death of many lost souls. God seems to play brinkmanship with history. Or, to put the point naturally rather than supernaturally, Plato seems to be right when he argues in book 10 of the *Republic* that the soul must be immortal because no matter how diseased souls can get, in vice and folly, they never are quite seen to die.

Second, the radical change we are now observing, the triumph of subjectivism, has not yet produced the "trousered ape". Even Hollywood movie magnates and proabortion feminists have some moral sense, though not quite as much as Mafia hit men. There were Sophists before — deniers of the natural law — and they remained human, as atheists remain human, and subject to religious categories. Those who deny sin remain sinners. Denial of what we are has never changed what we are before; why should it now?

Third, we see a counterattack beginning. We see ordinary people mounting a comeback against the evil "experts". Mere parents overcame massive media bias and powerful political pressure and successfully stopped the biggest public school system in America from imposing on first graders its propaganda for infidelity and sodomy, euphemistically called the "Rainbow Coalition". A few truly Catholic colleges have sprung up from the ruins of Judas' entrails. (Judas was the first Catholic who accepted a government grant.) Home schooling is skyrocketing. Organizations like Focus on the Family and Women for Faith and Family and Concerned Women for America, and the pro-life movement, are large and growing larger, despite a deliberate, dishonest media policy of censorship and vicious propaganda. The tide in the war for the human heart may be beginning to turn.

A fourth argument is an a priori one. A man without the natural law is not a man. A man without a heart is an oxymoron, neither ox nor moron, neither smart animal nor stupid human. Nothing can change its species. Man cannot become a "trousered ape" any more than he can become a trousered angel. He can become a bad man or a stupid man, but not an abolished man, except perhaps in Hell, where he loses his humanity and becomes "remains" for the ash pits of Gehenna. In this life you can only make an ass of yourself; in the next life, you can make an ash of yourself.

A fifth reason is an a fortiori argument. If even a demon-possessed man can be exorcised and returned to moral sanity, then that moral sanity must lie unabolished (though suppressed) beneath even demon possession. How much more, then, must it not lie unabolished beneath the decadent philosophies and practices of the modern world?

The sixth and clinching reason, I think, is from divine revelation, from what God has told us about himself and his actions: that he will not abandon us even if our world gets worse than Noah's world; that where sin abounds, grace does much more abound. He left us the rainbow as the first sign, and the cross as the second, of his promise never to abandon us entirely. He is our Father, after all, and the Father does not abandon his son, however prodigal. God lets his image in us get scratched, defaced, muddled, muddied, cracked, and forgotten—but never destroyed. Even the "Great Tribulation", we are assured, will be shortened, so that a remnant, at least, will be saved.

To complete Aquinas' case, let us briefly summarize the case for the opposition and imagine Aquinas' replies. That case consisted essentially of five arguments.

First, the example of actually existing men without consciences. Aquinas would reply that this is nothing new; that the "people of the lie" are no more shocking than Sardanopolis or Callicles or Thrasymachos.

Second, we have the genuinely new phenomenon of disbelief in the natural law among a whole culture, especially the intellectual establishments. Aquinas might answer simply that Western culture is no more the whole world than Roman culture was and that after the self-destruction of this culture, another will emerge, probably from the Third World.

Third, we seem to see the remarkable phenomenon of a selective slice of the natural law eliminated today: the sexual revolution. Many more people are much more radical here than anywhere else. Aquinas might reply that history shows more diversity in sexual beliefs and practices than in any other moral area already. Upper classes in ancient Athens and Rome were equally decadent. Let us not get so carried away playing the prophet that we think we are the first or worst decadents in history.

Fourth, if 2094 is to 1994 as 1994 is to 1894, we will be fully in a Brave New World long before 2094. This may be true, but it does not follow that the road will take no turning. History does not move linearly. It is not predictable. Man moves history before history moves men. And men choose and change. They even repent. When they do not, they are destroyed, like foreign substances in a body.

Fifth, there is the enormously increased technological power to change human nature and thought and behavior by genetic engineering and propaganda. The reply here is that our nuclear capability is equally radical. But the existence of such new powers does not necessarily mean their use.

There may be an invisible underground connection between these two new powers. It seems likely that if we grow wicked enough to eat the apple of genetic engineering, God will subject us to the severe mercy of nuclear death by our own hand to prevent Hell incarnate from reigning on earth. This would be a mordant twist to Aquinas' thesis, but it would still hold true.

Having heard the arguments on both sides, how shall we adjudicate them and declare the winner?

By the principle of inclusiveness. When there is evidence for two different hypotheses, the scientist always prefers the one that includes and explains the most data, especially if hypothesis A explains the data adduced as evidence for hypothesis B, but hypothesis B does not explain the data adduced as evidence for hypothesis A.

The pros, or the pessimists, do not and apparently cannot account for Aquinas' data nor refute his arguments, at least not as obviously as he can account for their data and refute their arguments. For his data are necessary principles, while theirs are changeable empirical observations. They adduce appearances, but behind appearances (like how fat your flesh is) lies a structured essence (like your skeleton) that is rigid and unchangeable.

Unless, of course, we are nominalists and these "essences" are mere mental inventions, while the empirical data are the "hard" data.

I have three final reasons for agreeing with Aquinas.

One is the argument from authority—not just of Aquinas but of nearly all the classical philosophers—and the saints to boot, e.g., Saint Thomas More assures us, "The times are never so bad but that a good man can live in them."

A second reason is the fact that Aquinas has an a priori argument— the unalterableness of a species or essence—while the other side has only a posteriori arguments. One certain a priori argument trumps many merely probable a posteriori arguments.

A third reason is that divine revelation trumps all human reason. God's past dealings with man are recorded in Scripture, and God's character as infinitely gracious, as revealed in Christ, is a more certain dam against the abolition of God's image in man (which includes the knowledge of the natural law) than any natural argument.

Finally, if the issue remains undecided by all argument, we can use William James' pragmatic test that he used to choose between free will and determinism, neither of which he thought theoretically provable. The pragmatic consequences of belief in free will justify that belief. And thus he freely chooses to believe in free choice. So here: let us freely choose to believe in the indestructibility of the natural law. When the mind remains uncertain, the heart, or the will to believe, can take over, by a reasonable kind of Pascalian wager. If we believe that the thing we are fighting to preserve, namely, the knowledge of the natural law in the heart of man, is indestructible and guaranteed eventual victory, we will fight joyfully and effectively and confidently. But if we believe that it is fragile, we will be driven by fear, anxiety, and pessimism, and our spiritual warfare will be less powerful, less joyful, and probably less saintly. So let us create our victory by believing in it. This is not New Age nonsense or a denial of epistemological realism. In sports, believing in yourself and your team is often a condition for victory. In religion, faith is a condition for salvation. Why should it not be a condition for the restoration of moral sanity to society? In the absence of proof, there is no reason not to choose hope.

But hope is not easy optimism. Our time is like the time of

Noah, and Lot, and Jezebel, and Diocletian. The fifties are over. Never again will American women's primary worry be waxy yellow buildup on the linoleum or ring around the collar — thank God! That was not the Kingdom but the Laodicean illusion. Our times may be terrible, even apocalyptic, but that is our normal situation according to Scripture: deadly peril, spiritual warfare, wrestling with principalities and powers in high places on earth and low places in Hell. Welcome back to East of Eden, Adam. Now perhaps you will believe again that the One who alone can save your society is the One who alone can save your soul.

5

Walker Percy's *Lost in the Cosmos:*
The Abolition of Man in
Late-Night Comedy Format

A scholarly essay, as everyone knows, should be: first, detailedly documented; second, fanatically footnoted; third, tightly textual; fourth, severely structured; fifth, soberly scientific; sixth, sternly serious; and seventh, deadly dull.

As you can probably guess by now, this is not going to be a scholarly essay.

I think I must have been reading too much Walker Percy, and have come down with one of his very communicable diseases: the disease of seeing our tragedies as comedies without ceasing to see them as tragedies. This is a disease (i.e., a *dis-ease*) that he seems to have caught from Euripides, Socrates, Aristophanes, Boccaccio, Shakespeare, Samuel Johnson, Pascal, Kierkegaard, and Chesterton.

But let's at least try to *begin* logically with some principles and definitions.

There are two ways to say what you want to say, or, as professors put it, two "communication modes": direct and indirect.

Humor is the most beloved kind of indirect communication. It is also often the most effective. It is nearly always the most memorable and repeatable.

There are three main theories of humor among philosophers (who are usually the most humorless humans haunting our planet). Darwinians see it as a nervous twitch, of the same genus as those of hyenas and eels. Marxists and Deconstructionists see it as class conflict, snide sneering, or social satire. Rationalists and classicists see it is incongruity, or irony: the contrast between appearance and reality.

Darwin and Marx having been pretty thoroughly discredited by now, let us assume the old Greeks were "onto something" (as Percy would say) when they saw irony as the metaphysical core of humor and apply this to Percy's use of it to communicate indirectly the same essential point Lewis communicated directly in *The Abolition of Man.*

Which is more effective, indirect or direct communication? That depends on the social situation and the receptivity of the audience. If the audience is rational and receptive, direct communication is more effective for two obvious reasons: it is *clearer* and it is *briefer.* For instance, Aristotle is clearer than Plato. (He is, of course, also duller and much less funny.) Aristotle says more things in less space. A Socratic dialogue — Plato's means of indirect communication — when compared with Aristotle lacks both clarity and brevity. It lacks clarity because it usually deliberately ends not with knowledge but with ignorance, or more exactly, with the reader's knowledge of his own ignorance. And it lacks brevity because Socrates takes thirty pages to get to a point that could be summarized in half a page by a professor or *Cliff Notes.* Yet the Socratic dialogue form has been read for twenty-four hundred years for much fun and profit — i.e., it has attained the two ends of all literature according to classical criticism, "to please and instruct" — and has done so more powerfully than any other form of communication in its field (philosophy).

There are two possible reasons why indirect communication sometimes works better than direct. Both reasons are features of the audience. First, the audience may be bored, jaded, skeptical, sleepy, and suspicious, i.e., the audience may be modern. (Percy points out that the very *word* "boredom" does not exist in any ancient language!) Second, the content of the message may be deeply threatening to the presuppositions, prejudices, or world view of the audience, so that a direct attack on these presuppositions would succeed only in eliciting bitterness, resentment, and defensiveness (or offensiveness), rather than open-minded thought, doubt, or questioning. This is usually what happens when Christians and non-Christians try to talk to each other about religion or anything religion makes a difference to, especially sex. Each side has its own religion and sees the other side as—well, The Other Side, "The Far Side".

Kierkegaard gave Percy the rationale for the method of indirect communication, especially in *The Point of View for My Work as an Author.* Kierkegaard faced this problem: how to dispel the religious illusion of the typically modern man. The illusion is that many people who think they are Christians are not, since the word no longer means something distinctive. They live in categories quite foreign to Christianity, the same categories as non-Christians ("aesthetic" categories of the interesting and the boring or, at most, ethical categories of duty to law rather than the essential Christian categories of sin versus faith). So the Christian writer must be a spy today. Kierkegaard's spy mission was to smuggle Christianity back into Christendom (nominally Christian civilization). Now a spy needs a cover. The Christian spy's best cover today is literary, or aesthetic—e.g., literary critic (C. S. Lewis), journalist (G. K. Chesterton), or novelist (Percy).

Lewis used both direct communication (in his nonfiction) and indirect communication (in his fiction). *The Abolition of Man* is direct communication, for it is the Riddell Memorial Lectures which he was *invited* to give. The same point of these lectures was made to a much wider audience *indirectly* in *That Hideous Strength,* for the audience that read that book was an audience that did not invite him, an audience whose world view he wanted to challenge.

So he used fiction. The Muslim proverb says: "Before you shoot the arrow of truth, dip it in honey." Indirect communication is honey.

There is also a middle form, halfway between fiction and nonfiction, which is also a form of indirect communication. This is the satirical essay, typified by Lewis' *Screwtape Letters* and Percy's *Lost in the Cosmos* (and, only a little less satirical, *The Message in the Bottle*).

The essential point of *Lost in the Cosmos* and the essential point of *The Abolition of Man* are essentially the same. Since these are two of my favorite books in the whole world; and since their common point is, it seems to me, the single most crucial issue and fateful choice facing Western civilization today, and therefore the whole human race, which is becoming increasingly Westernized; and since these two books typify the two communication forms; it seems a very right, proper, and obvious thing to compare them.

They are two of the six books of the twentieth century that I would make everyone on earth read if I were God. (A fine title for endless foolish ruminations: "If I were God . . . ") The other four would be Lewis' *Mere Christianity,* Chesterton's *The Everlasting Man* and *Orthodoxy,* and Huxley's *Brave New World.* Of the six, *The Abolition of Man* and *Lost in the Cosmos* fittingly come first as a precondition for the other four. For if the message of *The Abolition of Man* and *Lost in the Cosmos* (which is essentially that of objective values) is not heeded, if our civilization continues to drink what Lewis calls "the poison of subjectivism", it will become *Brave New World* and will lose all interest in, and eventually even comprehension of, the claims of Christianity, even when those claims are put as powerfully as Lewis and Chesterton put them in their other books. It will not refute them or even confute them, but it will blink blandly at them and classify them as an outdated lifestyle or a personal, subjective option. That is why Lewis says, in "The Poison of Subjectivism", that this master error, the subjectivity of values, "will certainly damn our souls and end our species". There can be no worse poison and no more important issue than that.

How do Lewis and Percy try to doctor the human soul that is drugged with the "poison of subjectivism"?

Since direct communication is clearer and simpler, let's look at *The Abolition of Man* first. This book is prophetic. It is couched in scholarly language (in fact, its plethora of learned Latinate references scare away even college students today, for this is the first generation in American history that is less well educated than its parents), but its content is a terrifying prophecy of mortality—not just the mortality of modern Western civilization (every sane person knows that, and many look forward to it as to the garbage collection) but the mortality of human nature itself if we do not recapture belief in the *Tao*.

Every civilization in human history has believed in the *Tao*. Ours is the first civilization in history that has abandoned the *Tao*, not just in practice (every civilization does that; it's called sin), but in theory, in belief. To the typically modern mind (and nothing more centrally defines the modern mind than this), objective reality no longer includes the moral dimension of good and evil. The "fact-value distinction" has become absolute. Facts do not include facts about values. Reality has been reduced to the scientific dimension of neutral, valueless fact. There is no longer anything outside ourselves and the products of our own minds to bow down to, conform to, or respect.

Even most traditionalists or conservatives do not see the radical, apocalyptic nature of this change as clearly as Lewis does. He shows that this is a true "transvaluation of all values" (Nietzsche), a 180-degree turn, a "turning the world upside down"—especially in the single most illuminating three sentences I have ever read about our civilization:

> There is something which unites magic and applied science [i.e., technology] while separating both from the 'wisdom' of earlier ages. For the wise men of old, the cardinal problem had

been how to conform the soul to reality, and the solution had been knowledge, self-discipline, and virtue. For magic and applied science alike the problem is how to subdue reality to the wishes of men: the solution is a technique.

Here the new *summum bonum* is contrasted with the old.

Technology is more like magic than like science. If you are surprised at this statement, you do not understand the essence of technology. Heidegger does: it is the fulfillment of the Nietzschean "will to power" as the new *summum bonum,* greatest good, or meaning and end of life. To see this point, imagine an experiment. Children are often given boxes to sort things in, and the observer can tell much about the children's minds by how they classify things. For instance, if a child is told to put a baseball, a basketball, a baseball bat, and a basketball net into two boxes, the "structuralist" or "static" child will put the two balls in one box and the two other items, which are not spheres, in the other box; the "functionalist" child will put the baseball and the bat in one box, and the basketball and its hoop in the other. Now suppose you are asked to classify four things—religion, science, magic, and technology—and to put them into two categories. Nearly everyone would classify science and technology together, and religion and magic together. There is a point to this classification: science and technology are limited to the empirically verifiable and the scientific method; religion and magic are not. But there is a deeper classification, and Lewis uses it. Science and religion both aim at conforming the mind to objective truth, objective reality (science conforms our mind to the nature of the universe, and religion conforms our mind to the mind of God and our will to the will of God). Magic and technology, on the other hand, try to conform objective reality to the human will. That is why they both arose at the same time—not the Middle Ages but the Renaissance, not the Age of God but the Age of Man. Both are Faustian, Promethean. The difference is, of course, that technology works while magic doesn't (usually). But their end, their goal, the purpose behind them, the human values and desires and state of soul that set them in motion, are the same.

The three main points of *The Abolition of Man* are summarized in the titles of its three chapters: (1) "Men without Chests", (2) "The Way", and (3) "The Abolition of Man".

1. Our civilization's educational elite, our opinion-molders (who have become much more powerful and much more philosophically radical since Lewis' day in each of the three main mind-molding establishments in our culture: education, entertainment, and journalism) are producing a new *species* of man: "men without chests", or hearts, or consciences—i.e., ears to hear the *Tao*. In other words, our "experts" are producing men and women like themselves. They are reproducing not biologically but culturally, by a kind of cultural cloning.

2. "The Way" or the *Tao* is the doctrine of (the existence and nature of) objective values, universal and unchangeable moral truths. Knowing the "way" made our ancestors human. Animals are amoral; men are moral or immoral.

3. "The abolition of man" will therefore necessarily follow if we continue to disbelieve and reject and forget the *Tao*. For the *Tao* is the precondition of our being human. Remove the cause or precondition and you remove the effect. Abolish the *Tao* and you abolish man. Become amoral and you become a clever ape, which is what current Darwinian orthodoxy believes you are anyway.

Another road to the same terrifying conclusion, "the abolition of man", is Lewis' exploration of "man's conquest of Nature" by technology. This new ideal of power over nature can only mean the *use* of nature as an instrument for the power of some men (the "Conditioners") over others (the "conditioned")—e.g., TV producers over their audiences, especially children and teenagers. Man is the last bit of nature to be conquered, and he will be conquered by *Tao*-less, naturalistic, amoral "Conditioners". Thus "man's conquest of Nature" turns out to be "Nature's conquest of man" and the "abolition of man". The equation "man's conquest of Nature" must be expanded at both ends, so that above the conquering "man" we see nature and under the conquered "nature" we see the conditioned men. (See diagram, p. 139.)

The first chapter ("Men without Chests") is the negative one; the second ("The Way") is the positive one, and the third ("The Abolition of Man") is the prophetic one. The first is the present, the second is the past, and the third is the future, if we keep sliding down the present slippery slope. The book is perfectly organized and complete, a work of art.

Walker Percy makes the same points, but in a different format. For while Lewis lectured to people who asked to be lectured at, nobody asked Percy. So he had to use the indirections of humor, satire, and irony to people who have learned to defend themselves against direct preachments of the *Tao* by singing Madonna's song "Papa, Don't Preach" instead of *the* Madonna's song "Be it done to me according to Thy word."

Lewis was lecturing to professionals, professors, and dons who may not have felt threatened by his jeremiads about modern Western civilization because they felt above it, abstracted from it, as its scholars, its historians, its professors—observers more than participants. They may not have been on Lewis' "side" philosophically, but they were on his "side" professionally, i.e., on the sidelines as members of the "observing class". Percy, on the other hand, talked to his fellow passengers on the *Titanic.* Lewis talked to his fellow officers. For Lewis was very British and Percy very American, and in England every passenger thinks he's some kind of officer, while in egalitarian America even the officers think of themselves as passengers.

But the message is the same. That message—the *Tao*—used to be The Primal Platitude. Now it's The Lost Secret. It used to be the map of the mainland, now it's "the message in the bottle". For like Crusoe we have been shipwrecked, lost, alienated from home.

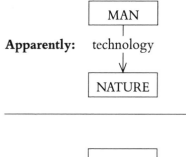

Apparently:

MAN

technology

NATURE

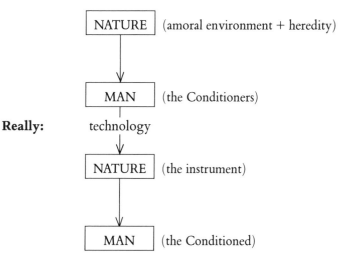

Really:

NATURE (amoral environment + heredity)

MAN (the Conditioners)

technology

NATURE (the instrument)

MAN (the Conditioned)

Any message from a world other than our island would come to us as Revelation. Any light that shines on our haunted wood would be a holy light.

For that is what our island is: a haunted wood. Our cosmos has become a haunted cosmos, *and we are the ghosts that haunt it.* That is Percy's answer in *Lost in the Cosmos* to the ancient oracle's puzzle "Know thyself."

Percy's "message in the bottle" is the gospel. The gospel is the good news about the Savior and Salvation. Salvation presupposes sin to be saved from. Sin presupposes the *Tao,* the objective moral law we sin against and which defines our sin as sin. ("Without the Law, I would not know sin as sin", says Saint Paul.) But modern man has been injected with "the poison of subjectivism" about values. Therefore the castaways who read the message in the bottle do *not* look up with joy and hope, but rather only say of that message, as of all messages, "It's only from us." *Everything* is "only from us" to the modern mind that rejects transcendence. Values too are "only from us", "our" values, "our" commandments, "our" rules, "our" games, "our" gods.

How can the Christian writer address such poor souls, such wraiths, such ghosts? There are only two ways: directly or indirectly, without or with a spy's cover; in scholarship or in satire; with pen or with pun; irenically or ironically. *The Abolition of Man* does the first, *Lost in the Cosmos* does the second. Same message, different medium.

Percy writes realistic novels about a world in which Lewis' prophecy has largely come true; a world of "men without chests", "trousered apes", walking clipboards, computers with hormones. In other words, our world. Camus said that future historians will need to say only two things of twentieth-century man: "He fornicated and read newspapers."

But this news is too "unacceptable" to announce directly. After so much evolutionary effort, man will not take kindly to the news that he is devolving back into the ape.

How then to play the prophet to the yuppie? Percy learned the technique from Kierkegaard, especially from *The Point of View for My Work as an Author,* in which he pointed out that the direct attack will no longer work because modern man has equipped himself with a new defensive weapon against it: boredom. The only thing modern man needs to do to protect himself against the radical infection of the gospel is to inoculate himself with a mild, boring version of it (i.e., exactly what we get in most Sunday sermons and Catholic theology departments), so as to build up antibodies against The Real Thing. Then he calls the prophet a "fanatic" and a "Fundamentalist" (his two new F-words) and simply ignores him.

But the Christian spy can still sneak into Christendom under cover of "the aesthetic" through indirection, irony, and wit. Then he doesn't seem serious or (therefore) threatening, although he really is both to an extreme degree.

Humor works like a spy slipping through the city gates while his partner distracts the guard. Like pickpockets—pickpockets always work in twos. One distracts, the other picks. Humor slips in the "zinger", the punch line, during that infinitesimally short moment of mental silence and defenselessness when the chattering, ideologically propagandized ego has its defenses down and doesn't know what it's supposed to think or say. All great humor works in this holy silence, this window of opportunity.

The gospel too comes in silence, works on the soul only in silence. Just as it was in the silence of midnight, when all things were hushed, that the Eternal Word leaped down from Heaven, so it is in the silence of the heart that the Word rushes in. Kierkegaard knew this well. Many times he wrote something like this:

> If I were a doctor, and I were allowed to prescribe only one remedy for all the ills of the modern world, I would prescribe silence. For even if the Word of God were proclaimed in the modern world, it would be choked to death with noise, it would not be heard, because there is no silence. Therefore, create silence.

Humor does that, humor creates silence. And in this silence, as the ego sleeps, the Eternal Word slips like Santa down your chimney.

God did what Kierkegaard and Percy did: he used irony and indirect communication and even humor in his biggest punch line. When he revealed himself most definitively, he didn't come with blare of trumpets to the Emperor's throne but with the lowing of cows to an animal feeding trough. He didn't come to Rome but to Bethlehem. He did not shape the sky into a gigantic mouth, but he came as a spy who created his own cover: the cover of a poor baby. The Incarnation is the most ironic thing that ever happened, and if you are on the wavelength of ironic humor, the most hilarious trick ever played (except perhaps the even greater one thirty-three years later when he did the Devil in with his own judo on the Cross).

There was a TV comedy show some years ago called "Steam Bath", in which God was a worldly-wise, street-smart Puerto Rican janitor in the locker room of a steam bath between worlds. The real story is no less incredible and no less ironic: God as an apolitical Jewish carpenter who got crucified for blasphemy and treason.

In *Fear and Trembling,* Kierkegaard distinguished "the knight of faith", the Christian hero, from "the knight of infinite resignation", the classical pagan hero. "The knight of faith" is ordinary, like a carpenter. "The knight of infinite resignation" is extraordinary and obvious and aloof, like a king. God himself became a hero of his own faith. Kierkegaard wrote, "If God had willed to appear as a gigantic green bird sitting on a high hill and whistling in an unheard-of manner, then even our bored society man would be the first to notice." That would be direct communication. But that would set up a false relationship. It would be the true God, but untruly related to man. Kierkegaard, like Percy, is more concerned with truth in the *relationship* with God than with truth in the *concepts* about God. The false relationship that a direct communication would set up, according to Kierkegaard (in *Fear and*

Trembling and also in *Concluding Unscientific Postscript*) is the relationship of "immediacy", the relationship between the unambiguously divine and the amazed, stunned, passive, and unfree observer. Instead, God wants to set up the true relationship of free choice, trust, and love. To do this, the direct relationship must be avoided. God must speak indirectly instead. He must disguise himself, like a spy, like the king disguising himself as a humble peasant boy in order to woo the humble peasant maiden (in Kierkegaard's beautiful allegorical fairy tale in chapter 2 of *Philosophical Fragments*).

This is the answer, by the way, to one of the simplest and hardest of all objections against Christianity, the question C. S. Lewis wrote *Till We Have Faces* to answer: Why doesn't God reveal himself more clearly? "Why must holy places be dark places?" In Bertrand Russell's words, "Why didn't You give us more *evidence?*" (That's the question he said on his deathbed he would ask God if he found out after death that God existed after all!) The answer to this question is in Lewis' title *Till We Have Faces.* The answer is: "How can God meet us face to face till we have faces?" How can the king marry the maiden happily until she is brought to equality with him somehow, so that she can see him face to face and not die? In order to lift her up, the king lowers himself down—the *kenosis,* the emptying.

So Percy does what God did. He descends. He becomes a modern skeptic, or a "bad Catholic", like Dr. Tom More—someone very unlike his favorite saint, *Saint* Thomas More—so that he can inveigle us Toms to more. Percy speaks not through heroes but antiheroes, not saints but sinners, not beautiful people but people only a little less grotesque than Flannery O'Connor's grotesqueries.

The strategical reasoning is as follows. He wants to address the ironic fact that modern man, who thinks he's "with it", is really "out of it". So he speaks through people who are apparently "out of it", like the wacky old priest in the tower in *The Thanatos Syndrome*—a modern Simeon Stylites, probably the least comprehensible and sympathetic saint possible to modern man. For in a world which confuses "with it" with "out of it" because its "it" is man's fashion instead of God's eternity, "with it" and "out of it" are exactly reversed. Percy stands us on our heads because this is the only way to put us right side up. We are already standing on our heads, upside down, with our eyes in the mud and dirt and earth, and our nose to the grindstone, and our heels kicking rebelliously up against the heavens (to use one of Chesterton's thousands of unforgettable images). So, like Chesterton, Percy turns everything upside down. To do this, he first stands on his head too, alongside modern man. But he *knows* he's upside down.

Kierkegaard used the same strategy by adopting pseudonyms for the non-Christian points of view from which he wrote many of his books, creating fictional authors for his philosophy instead of fictional characters for a story. For instance, "Johannes de Silento", John the Silent, is the objective Socratic observer who is amazed at Abraham in *Fear and Trembling.* "Johannes Climacus", John the Climber, compares the Socratic and the Christian standpoints in *Philosophical Fragments* from a Socratic rather than a Christian point of view, thereby revealing more about what Christianity adds to philosophical wisdom than any direct Christian preaching could do.

The heart of irony is the contradiction between "what seems" and "what is", between appearance and reality. This distinction is the origin of both philosophy and science, for both philosophy and science presuppose the questioning of appearances to find the hidden reality—something neither animals nor computers do. Animals and computers cannot be ironic.

Kierkegaard and Jesus are Percy's two main models for irony. Kierkegaard wrote his doctoral dissertation on "The Concept of Irony". And Jesus' humor, like most Jewish humor, centered on irony. So Percy's does too, especially in *Lost in the Cosmos.*

Irony is the subtlest and highest (most divine) form of humor. He that sitteth in the heavens laughing is not relieving his nervous tensions, or needing a comic relief from an onerous life, or sneeringly enjoying other people's discomfort, or tittering at erotic suggestions. All these theories of humor fail because they don't go to its profoundest root, which must be rooted in God somehow. (Everything good is.) God is an ironist. God is even a punster. (Puns are linguistic ironies.) For he created a world where one thing means many other things, like a pun. Meaning in the God-created universe is multi-dimensional. As von Balthasar puts it, "truth is symphonic". The only unambiguous, univocal, non-ironic, unfunny language is mathematics. (Computers have no sense of humor.)

Indeed, the fundamental pun is the word "being" itself. It is analogical, not univocal. Creatures only borrow being, God *is* being. It is also double: essence and existence. These two fundamental technical theses of Thomistic metaphysics are puns on the word "being". It is almost like defining "being" as "what bees do" — only Thomas' two puns on "being" are much more subtle and all-encompassingly true.

God is Jewish. Therefore his universe is full of Jewish humor, Jewish ironies. Many people "just don't get" Jewish humor, just as some people "just don't get" English humor. Both are too subtle and ironic, in different ways. Crude and dull minds want *jokes,* not irony. They want tension-relievers, occasions to feel superior, or erotic teases. God and Percy prefer the humor of profound play, the delighted juggling of the ambiguities of being.

One of my most traumatic teaching memories was the first time I assigned *Lost in the Cosmos* with no introductions or explanations and asked for feedback. Most of the students just didn't understand that the book was supposed to be funny! They took it seriously as a self-help book, instead of a parody on self-help books, and gave straight answers to all the quiz questions! This happened before Percy died. I thought of sending him my students' reactions, but I didn't, because I feared it would cause a clinical depression or a heart attack and a premature death. Maybe somebody else did; maybe that's why he died.

Percy's humor is Jewish, even though he isn't, except in spirit. Perhaps deep down every good comedian is Jewish, as every good cook is French, every good philosopher is Greek, and every good lover is Italian. Like Pascal (another one of his deepest influences), Percy was deeply impressed by the uniqueness of the Jews and their history. He says in *The Thanatos Syndrome* that modern media have cheapened and flattened the language and emptied out the bite from every other word except the word "Jew". It is the only word that has not had its teeth pulled. Other words have become putty. They can mean anything the manipulators (Lewis' "Conditioners") make them mean, like the disembodied little squiggles on a computer screen. But the word "Jew" remains scandalously concrete and unassimilated, like the Jews themselves. They are the alternative to the Tower of Babble.

Only the Word can save us from the Tower of Babble. The Jews and the Greeks prepared for the Word. Jewish wisdom, in humor as well as in the prophets, is a natural preparation for the Word made flesh; Greek wisdom, in drama and philosophy, is too. Jewish humor, Jewish prophecy, Greek drama, and Greek philosophy are all ironic. All four sharply distinguish appearance and reality.

Daniel Bell, the famous Harvard educator (and a Jew himself) describes Jewish humor thus:

> Jewish humor is not jokes. A joke is a contrived situation, a manipulated effect, a commodity of the moment. Jewish humor is wit, the play of words, the compression of language to reflect the compression chamber of life. [For instance:] Two men stand outside Lubiyanka, the old dungeon in Moscow. The two stand there, not saying a word. Eventually, one of them gives a long sigh. And the other says, agitatedly, 'Yankel, how many times am I telling you not to discuss politics here?'

Irony, the heart of Jewish humor, is the clash between appearance and reality. The humor questions the appearances, even the most apparently obvious truism in the world, the Law of Non-contradiction:

> A rabbi held court, hearing two women with complaints against each other. The rabbi listened intently to the first and, persuaded by her tears, said, 'You are right.' The other woman protested: 'Wait, you have not heard me.' The rabbi listened to her and, again persuaded, said: '*You* are right.' The rabbi's wife, perplexed, said: 'How can they both be right?' And the rabbi said to her, 'You are right too.'

Another example of overcoming logic itself: Sidney Morgenbesser, a Jewish philosopher at Columbia, was confronted at Oxford by John Austin, the British logician, who said to him, "Mr. Morgenbesser, I am told that you believe that two affirmatives can make a negative. Now that is just not possible in English. In our language, two negatives can make an affirmative, but two affirmatives cannot make a negative." To which Morgenbesser replied, "Yeah, yeah."

Lost in the Cosmos views the world with this kind of ironic humor and uses the gentle mouthpiece of the ironist to deliver the terrifyingly serious point that Lewis delivers "straight" in *The Abolition of Man.* The mouthpiece is in many ways similar to that of late-night comedy, especially the beloved Johnny Carson and David Letterman. Both these comedians are gentle ironists, in the Will Rogers tradition. Both find humor in situations, in conversations. They don't tell *jokes.* They're not standup comics with artificial routines. They find the humor *in* the real human situation, and that humor is largely irony. Though both are Gentiles, they share much of the world and life view of Jewish humor. Let us take two examples that must have influenced Percy at least unconsciously.

Perhaps the most well loved, memorable, and funny of Carson's characters was Carnak the Magnificent. Carnak gave questions to others' answers instead of vice versa, thus applying ironic reversal to the very situation and format of questioning. Question-and-answer humor is typically Jewish. The rabbis, like Socrates, taught by questioning rather than just by answering. Jewish humor, like Socratic philosophy, usually begins with a question and ends with a surprise answer, a turnaround, an irony. An archetypal example: "Why does a Jew always answer a question with another question?" "Why *shouldn't* a Jew answer a question with another question?" The two greatest teachers in history did that all the time: Jesus and Socrates.

Carnak's reversing of questions and answers is paralleled by the most oft-quoted of all the rabbinical questions: "God is the answer, but what is the question?" That question is the theme of one of the most beautiful fairy tales ever written, and perhaps the most profoundly Christian, "The Golden Key" by George MacDonald. A boy and a girl find a golden key, but they have to search all worlds for the door it opens. They get the answer first, then they look for the question. Like Carnak. Like us. For the answer, the golden key, is Christ. This answer has been dumped into our laps, into our world. Now we have to rearrange and reinterpret our lives around this answer. We have to rearrange our questions. Our fundamental situation is hilariously ironic: millions of people milling around looking not for the key but for the door, not for the answer but for the question. Like Carnak. And like modern man, lost in the cosmos, with thousands of little answers to little questions about the cosmos, but lacking the fundamental question (much less the answer) "Know thyself." Socrates' question.

Lost in the Cosmos does not aim to give the reader a better answer, but (Socratically) it inveigles him to ask a better question than the one he is asking, to pose the great puzzle about himself. Why does the astronomer know more about a galaxy than about the astronomer?

The question is a trick question, an unanswerable question, a *koan.* For the self can't be known as an object of knowledge, since it is not an object but a subject. That's what a self means: an "I". That's God's great joke on us: we're eyes that can see everything except themselves, mirrors that can reflect everything in the universe except themselves. And yet that is precisely our one essential task: to find ourselves.

If this is so, the logical corollary is then that either the self cannot be known—ever—or else that it can be known only by another, higher self. Only to the Absolute Subject can human subjects be objects. "The message in the bottle"—divine revelation— can tell us who we are if and only if it's *not* "only from us". The failure of naturalistic, secularistic modern psychologies of self-knowledge and (correlatively) self-help, laid bare by Percy's satire in *Lost in the Cosmos,* clears the way for our receptivity to the alternative, listening to divine revelation and divine salvation, the two things modern man needs most and wants least. You can't feed him that spinach directly. (Ever tried to feed a baby spinach? You have to trick him.) Only if you distract his attention, tell a joke, or tickle him can you get some spinach down in that golden window of opportunity while he's stopped to be silent and then laugh.

Just as most viewers love and remember Carson's Carnak the best, they love and remember Letterman's lists the best. *Lost in the Cosmos* is full of lists, most of them in the form of simple or elaborate multiple-choice questions, in which all the answers are partly right. What is so significant about lists? Lists are like road maps; they artificially separate, analyze, order, and quantify things. The ancient habit of dividing things into lists—The Twelve Steps to Mystical Experience, The Four Last Things, The Seven Wonders of the World, The Four Noble Truths—is a precursor of the analytic, scientific mind. But analysis and quantification are precisely what you can never do with the self, the "I", the single subject that unifies all the objects in our experience into a single world, as the narrator of a novel unifies all the ingredients into one novel, the object of his consciousness.

That's why the word "psychology" is literally an oxymoron. "Logy" means "science", and "science" means analysis and quantification, and the psyche or self is precisely what *does* all analyzing and quantifying. It can no more be analyzed or quantified than light can be lit up, or a mirror appear as an object in a mirror. (Only the frame or boundary of a mirror can appear in a mirror, and only the frame or boundaries of the self can appear as an object to the self.)

Pop psychology is full of lists, step-by-step programs, ways of climbing Jacob's ladder rung by rung from the bottom up, from psychological purgatory or earth to psychological heaven, from neurosis to homeostasis, from alienation to adjustment, from Victorian repression or Christian moralism to "free expression" and "sexual fulfillment", from being wronged to asserting your rights, from Fundamentalism or fanaticism to becoming a good member of the Kingdom of This World.

But what can't be climbed by steps or lists is the true Jacob's ladder, the ladder to Heaven—even the heaven of your true self. The only way that ladder can go anywhere is upside down. The true Jacob's ladder is the exact opposite of the Tower of Babel: not an erection but a descent, not Promethean but kenotic, incarnational. Babel collapses in babble, but Jacob's ladder holds even angels. Finally, it holds the Word himself, the healer of Babel's babble. He himself says so, identifies himself as the real Jacob's ladder. (Compare John 1:51 with Genesis 28:12.)

Today, Babel's babble is psychobabble. Pop psychology is our most popular Tower, our new religion, both inside and outside the Church. Self-help books of psychology outnumber all other science books in bookstores. And even in the Church, more people, including clergy, look to psychology than to theology and see Jesus as the original Mister Rogers and the Church as Mister Rogers' Neighborhood. (A friend of mine swears he even heard an Easter sermon whose point was that Jesus' message from the Cross was "I'm O.K., you're O.K." I wonder how all that blood crept into the story?)

Such a situation calls for satire, not fulmination. But the problem is serious (as well as comic). The problem is simply that all our

Babels just don't work. No ladder will stretch as far as we all want to go. Our hearts remain restless until they rest in him, despite all of our "peace of mind" prophets who proclaim "peace, peace" when there is no peace.

Deep down we're all divinely discontent with this wonderful but fallen world and this defaced masterpiece that is the human self, the self that produces both martyrs and murderers. Even those who don't believe in Heaven don't really believe in earth either, deep down. That's why they tell jokes about it; you don't tell jokes about your faith.

They long to know the answer to Patti Page's great question, "Is That All There Is?" And they wonder how to get there if there *is* something more. The situation of the secularist is exactly that of the archetypal Maine farmer joke: "Ye cain't git there from here."

No, you can't. You can't know your final end by yourself. You can't even know yourself by yourself. The self is a *koan,* a puzzle that is unsolvable in principle — like "tell me the somebody you were when you were nobody." *Only God can know you.* The secret of your identity is in your Author alone because you are his character. Only transcendence can know you. And only transcendence can save you. Jacob's ladder works only because God makes it; it comes down from Heaven.

Jacob's ladder is, of course, Jesus Christ. Walker Percy is a kind of modern John the Baptist, especially in *Lost in the Cosmos,* preparing the way for the gospel, exalting valleys and flattening hills, exalting publicans and flattening pharisees, exalting shlemiels and flattening shmucks, "comforting the afflicted and afflicting the comfortable", in Dorothy Day's words. The true King is coming and wants to enter his throne room of the self; but the road is full of big chunks of psychobabble. *Lost in the Cosmos* is palm branches to cover the bullshit. It is a pooper-scooper for psychobabble.

The central irony in this book is that the human self that has finally learned so many of the secrets of the cosmos has forgotten the thing closest to itself. The more we know, the less we know *who* it is who knows it all.

William Barrett in *Irrational Man* puts this ironic point in two sentences which, when rubbed together like flint and steel, produce a spark, an enlightening question. Point one: modern man has exhaustively studied everything, especially himself. He has not ignored himself. On the contrary, our most popular science is psychology. Nothing has been more mapped and studied than the self in modern times. Point two: yet after all this effort we know ourselves far *less* than we ever did before. The more we know *about* ourselves, the less we know ourselves. What could be more ironic?

How did this happen?

There are two answers. The most important one is that we have forgotten God. We no longer believe what we have been told about ourselves from our creator and designer. The character has forgotten who he is because he has thrown away the script and rejected the playwright. This can and must be changed. We can and must return, repent, convert. But there is a second reason for the paradox which cannot be undone. It lies in the very nature of the self and the nature of knowledge and takes a little explanation.

Where English has only one word for "know", German and French have two: *kennen* and *wissen, connaître* and *savoir.* They are inversely proportional; the more we know in one way, the less we know in the other. The more object knowledge, the less subject knowledge. The more analysis, the less synthesis. The more quantity, the less quality. (That principle seems to hold true for our whole world.) The more left brain, the less right brain. The more rational, the less intuitive. The more masculine, the less feminine. Karl Stern says our whole modern Western civilization is in a "Flight from Woman". So we naturally call it "feminism".

We know the cosmos of objects by objective, rational knowledge, by science. We know ourselves only by intuitive knowledge. Prescientific ancients often made the mistake of trying to know the cosmos by intuition, myth, poetry, and mysticism instead of science. We moderns usually make the far deadlier error of trying to understand the self by science. They personalized the universe; we depersonalize the self. They thought even matter was spirit; we think even spirit is matter. They thought even things were persons; we think even persons are things. They worshipped the earth as the body of a god; we call psychology a science. Which mistake is more stupid and deadly?

Since rational and intuitive knowledge are mutually exclusive (at least at the same time) and inversely proportionate, since you must sacrifice the one (at least temporarily) to do the other right, a surprising corollary follows: there is no such thing as total and simple progress. Every progress is also a regress. Each step forward is also a step back. Thought works by a law similar to the law of matter, that for each action there must be an equal and opposite reaction. There's no free lunch, except for God, who can create something out of nothing without it reacting on him and know it without it influencing him (until he becomes one of us and hangs on a cross and takes our reactions straight in the heart).

The religion of progress is dying. The "enlightenment" (i.e., the Great Darkness) is almost as dead as Communism, which was one of its children. No reasonable person believes in salvation through science and technology anymore, just as nobody believes in salvation by the all-encompassing State anymore, except the Democratic party, humanities departments in prestigious American universities, and the sages who tell lies in our newspapers and addict us to lust, greed, and violence on TV. (One gets the image of desperately optimistic Englishmen sniffing the air aboard the *Titanic* as it lists at a 45-degree angle, and comfortably conversing: "Lovely voyage, wot? What nice progress we're making!")

Everyone else knows the obvious: modernity is a disaster. The only people you can still fool about that are the professors, the world's most pampered people. Real people know darn well that nearly everything called progress in society is really regress. (Science and technology is another matter, a spectacular success story of knowledge and power, but hardly happiness—except in medicine.) When a developer destroys a beauty spot, we say, "Oh, well, you can't stop progress." When marriages and families are destroyed by antireligious and antimoral philosophies of selfishness, we call it modern "Realism". When public schools confiscate Bibles and distribute condoms, recruit for sodomy but outlaw prayer, the answer to popular parental protest is that they are "religious right-wing extremists, who want to turn back the clock and restore the Inquisition". How long before free drugs and bordellos in high schools? The "progress" from McGuffey to Dewey is already much greater than from Dewey to the Brave New World. We're three-fourths of the way there.

But if Percy said it *that* way no one would review him and almost no one would know about him. So he has to fool the critics with a cover: indirection, irony, humor, the prophet's cover in a world that's a nonprophet organization. So he hides his bomb in the subtitle to *Lost in the Cosmos:* "The Last Self-Help Book"— that is, the self-help book to end all self-help books, the self-refuting, self-destroying self-help book.

If self-help is futile, only God can save us. Percy does not preach the second point, but he shows the first. If modern man does not believe the first point, he will not be in the market for the second. Therefore Percy does a more important work for the salvation of souls and society than the preachers do. He softens up the ground for their seed.

C. S. Lewis makes the same point as Percy about modern psychology and its ugly little sister sociology also by indirection in his fiction, most clearly through a minor character in *That Hideous Strength,* Hingest, a chemist, who is the only real scientist in the book. He had joined the demonic N.I.C.E. because he thought it had something to do with science, but left because he found that it was instead all about applied psychology and sociology and ideology. His words come in response to something Mark Studdock said about "sciences like sociology": "There *are* no sciences like sociology. You can't know people. You can only get to know them."

That's the distinction: *kennen* versus *wissen, connaître* versus *savoir.* Knowing people as you know statistical patterns of behavior, or brain chemistry, or genes, or diets, is impossible. You know them in a fundamentally different way from the way you know things because they have a fundamentally different kind of being from things. They are "thous", not "its", subjects, not objects. You know them by *sophia,* by wisdom, not by *cogito,* by cogitation.

Ever since Descartes, we've idealized *cogito* as the most perfect kind of knowledge. But all attempts to grasp ourselves by *cogito* have failed. And now we are the Great Unknown, we knowers of all things. We are "lost in the cosmos".

The reason we're "lost in the cosmos" is because we are not in the cosmos in the first place. That's Percy's point: we subjects transcend the cosmos, the sum of all objects. Objectively and physically, the cosmos swallows us up like a flea; as subjects, we spiritually contain the universe.

Lewis puts the same startling point in chapter 3 of *Miracles:* that human consciousness is not part of nature, not one of the many objects that make up the universe. It is literally supernatural. For *the knowledge of a thing is not one of the thing's parts.* Therefore the knowledge of nature (which we have) cannot be a part of nature.

Percy also says this under a second spy cover, the cover of semiotic scientist, in the central section of *Lost in the Cosmos.* The clearest behavioral difference between man and animals is language. Animals have only signals, man has signs. The additional factor — "the delta factor" — is meaning, or concept, or word. *Logos* means all three of these things in Greek: the objective meaning or essence, the idea which understands it, and the word which expresses it. Without *logos,* no humanity. "In the beginning was the Word" (*Logos*) for humanity too. Helen Keller became functionally human the day she discovered, down by the well, that one thing *means* another, that words signify, that a word is a thing that is also a sign.

Husserl called this phenomenon "intentionality"—that strange feature of ideas and words by which they *point.* Animals don't understand pointing, signs, or significance. Point to a beautiful sunset and the animal will sniff your finger, not follow it to the sunset.

This is the very essence of language, and this is the very thing that our newest and most fashionable philosophy, Deconstructionism, denies: that the words, or the text, mean something beyond themselves. Texts are only texts, things. There's no difference between text and world. There's no intelligible real world out there, just word games. A hall of mirrors. It's all text.

I'm sure that if Lewis had lived to see Deconstructionism, he would have agreed with Percy in calling it utterly nihilistic and dehumanizing, perhaps even apocalyptic. For Deconstructionism turns Helen Keller the significance-reading girl back into Helen the animal, playing physical, arbitrary games with meaningless signals. Helen, the discoverer of the world of spirit, is turned into Helen "the material girl".

Archibald MacLeish wrote in *Ars Poetica* that "a poem must be palpable and mute/ Like globed fruit. . . . A poem must not mean, but be." He may have meant only that poetry shouldn't moralize, but it certainly sounds like Deconstructionism: words (meanings) reduced to things. Reductionism versus transcendence.

Reductionism is what Lewis warns against also in *The Abolition of Man.* Lewis fights the battle mainly in the moral arena, Percy in the cognitive and linguistic arena. In *The Abolition of Man,* the reduction of the transcendent, supernatural *Tao* to man-made conventions and the correlative reduction of the instrument for detecting this *Tao,* the "chest" or heart or moral sentiment or conscience, to instinct or social utility—this makes man into an un-man, like Weston in *Perelandra.* To put it simply, it destroys the soul. Souls are only *physically* indestructible. They are morally and spiritually vulnerable and destructible. That is what Hell is. "Fear not him who is able only to destroy the body; fear him who is able to destroy both body and soul in Hell" (Mt 10:28).

The two things that distinguish man from the beast are *Logos* and *Tao,* the word and the law, understanding and morality. Abolish both and you abolish man and get "trousered apes"; you abolish Socrates and get Phil Donahue.

Is it possible for man to be abolished? Can evolution be reversed? Why not? There is more of a philosophical problem with evolution than with devolution. The philosophical problem with evolution is that it violates the principle of causality unless there is a God directing the process, for you can't get more out of less. Primordial slime by itself can't turn into chickens and cavemen and lawyers. (Well, maybe lawyers. . . .) But it could easily work the other way. You can get less out of more. Why couldn't devolution happen? Why couldn't a few men start swinging through trees instead of walking on two feet, and go naked and eat bananas, and develop the habit and pass it on to their children, and gradually devolve into apes? (Better yet, forget the trees: just feed your mind with newspapers and the boob tube.)

The ancients thought this could not happen. I hope they were right, but I'm not sure. Saint Thomas Aquinas argued that "the natural law can never be abolished from the heart of man" (S. T. I–II, 94, 6). Perhaps if Saint Thomas had seen the Clarence Thomas confirmation hearings, he may have had second thoughts.

Suppose he did. What would Saint Thomas have thought of Judge Thomas and those who judged him? Let's try to imagine it.

The setting is Judge Thomas being judged as fit or unfit to be a Supreme Court Justice by Senator Ted Kennedy, the "Saint of Chappaquiddick". (This is before the Anita Hill brouhaha erupted and restored the good Judge's spunk and spleen.) As you listen, note Judge Thomas' desperate dance to escape the fearsome and damning accusation that—he actually believes in that utterly unacceptable, terrifyingly traditional, cancerously conservative, totally-non-PC idea of the natural law—that is, that he, a justice, dares to believe in a real *justice!*

KENNEDY: Judge Thomas, in your writings you have left behind you a trail of opinions, sort of like a snail leaving a trail of slime. It glows. It's very easy to follow. Why, even I can follow it. And a prominent part of that opinion trail is your words of praise for certain writers who advocated—right out there in print, in public, in the naked light of day, where we could see it and sneer at them—a (*choke! spit!*) "natural law"! (*Rolls his head in expression of holy horror.*)

THOMAS: Well, now, Senator, really, now, I think I only meant to say, or meant to think, or thought to mean . . . uh, I mean I only tried to encourage those conservatives to work harder for civil rights, that's all. "Natural law" was just a funny way of saying "civil rights".

KENNEDY: Then why did you say "natural law" instead of just "civil rights"?

THOMAS: Well, you know, all that language was . . . just . . . well . . .

KENNEDY (*helpfully*): Vague, irresponsible speculation by a part-time amateur philosopher talking through his hat and not to be taken at all seriously? Is that it?

THOMAS: Thank you, Senator! That's it. That's it exactly. I couldn't have put it better myself. Thank you, Senator. I compliment your accuracy. You went to Harvard, didn't you? I'm a Yalie, you know. Say, did you pull yourself up by your own bootstraps to get to Harvard, as I did to get to Yale?

KENNEDY: We didn't have bootstraps.

THOMAS: What?

KENNEDY: We had no affirmative action for the Irish, you know. All we had was Daddy's millions.

THOMAS: You know, that reminds me. Can I tell you the story one more time about how my grandfather worked twenty hours a day crushing pea pods in his backyard?

KENNEDY: Judge, we've heard that story half a dozen times already. What we really want to know is whether you believe there's some mysterious higher law above the laws enacted by the good people of this great nation of Massachusetts—excuse me, I mean America— something . . . something . . . (*spitting out the word reluctantly, with horror*) *religious?*

THOMAS: Well, you know, I have a soft spot in my heart for the nuns who taught me . . .

KENNEDY: That's not what I'm asking. Do you believe there's something . . . religious (*wipes his mouth*) above the will of the people?

THOMAS: What people, Senator?

KENNEDY: Why, *the* people, of course. People who think like me.

THOMAS: What about people who don't think like you?

KENNEDY: Wait a minute, here. Stop being impertinent. I'm supposed to be making a fool of you here, not vice versa.

THOMAS: Well, go ahead and do your thing, then.

KENNEDY: Come clean and clear, Judge. Are you telling me that you really don't believe in this cockamamie natural law thing after all? Do you agree now with all of us good people that there can be no higher law than the law of the Reich—I mean, the State? You did praise some defenders of natural law in print.

THOMAS: I'm sorry, Massah. Please don't punish me. I promise I won't do it again.

KENNEDY: Well, I should hope not. Because it's . . . it's . . . it's downright . . .

THOMAS (*helpful*): Fascistic? Nazi? Dictatorial?

KENNEDY: Worse. It's . . . *inappropriate!*

THOMAS: Say *what?*

KENNEDY: Didn't you ever watch "Mister Rogers' Neighborhood" when you were little?

THOMAS: No, we didn't have a TV.

KENNEDY: But you've seen the show?

THOMAS: Oh, yes.

KENNEDY: Then try to imagine me as Mister Rogers. These hearings are my neighborhood. And in my neighborhood, we just don't say dirty words like "natural law", because they're *inappropriate.* Now—can you say "inappropriate"? It's a big word, twice as big as "natural". Let's see if you can say it with me. "Inappropriate."

THOMAS: "Inappropriate."

KENNEDY: Good boy! You know, if you keep practicing, and performing well, and jumping through all my hoops, then maybe I'll even *like you just the way you are!*

Question for Group Discussion: Do you think that if John the Baptist had been able to watch Mister Rogers when he was a little kid prophet, he would have learned to like Herod just the way he was?

The "trousered apes" produced by the abolition of the *Tao* may sound funny and even harmless when satirized, but the issue is more deadly serious than a nuclear holocaust. For bombs can only destroy bodies, but philosophies can destroy souls.

(For some strange reason nobody is worried about nuclear war anymore—as if the world suddenly became saintly when the U.S.S.R. suddenly became defunct, and as if Gorbachev was more likely to start one than some little crackpot dictator who steals some plutonium and buys that book the U.S. Government refused to censor—the book by a University of Minnesota physics student that tells you how to build your own nuclear bomb for $200 with materials you can buy in public supply stores.)

Here is the terrifying passage in *Lost in the Cosmos* that explains the connection between *Tao*-lessness and violence (also sex):

> The Self since the time of Descartes has been stranded, split off from everything else in the Cosmos, a mind which professes to understand bodies and galaxies but is by the very act of understanding marooned in the Cosmos, with which it has no connection. It therefore needs to exercise every option in order to reassure itself that it is not a ghost but is rather a self among other selves. One such option is a sexual encounter. Another is war. The pleasure of a sexual encounter derives not only from physical gratification but also from the demonstration to oneself that, despite one's own ghostliness one is, for the moment at least, a sexual being. Amazing! Indeed, the most amazing of all the creatures in the Cosmos: a ghost with an erection!

Mention of war here takes the fun out of the joke. Why do we connect sex with violence? Because both are often motivated by our need to prove that we are not ghosts.

This is no longer funny. Drunks are funny from a distance but certainly not in your family. All of Western civilization is one family, and it is full of drunks. They write most of the scripts.

What can we do? "What shall I do to be saved?" (Acts 16:30)—the only really serious question.

Lewis and Percy offer the same solution. For there is only one. When you make a mistake, there is no hope in "progress", no hope in just going on. There is hope only in regress, in repentence. You must go back to where you turned off the right road and somehow find your way back onto it. Only then can you progress. You must do what the very essence of modernism says cannot be done; you must turn back the clock. You must murder your new god, the idol Progress. You must repent to be saved.

This is not doom. Both authors are optimistic. It *can* be done. We are free to make this choice.

Lewis ends *The Abolition of Man* on a note of hope, not doom. He says that even from science itself, the cure for scientism and reductionism may come through a new, antireductionistic science. In other words, we can still make real progress and move from Skinner to Aristotle.

Percy also sings a note of hope in *Lost in the Cosmos,* even in his most apocalyptic and frightening scenario in the book. The last space ship from earth, carrying the last surviving members of the species whose inherent death wish and violence had destroyed the earth, reaches Alpha Centauri and asks permission from the inhabitants of that planet to land there. The Alpha Centaurians reply that they must first judge the danger earthmen may pose to their own planet—they must determine which category of intelligence earthlings fit into. They have found that the cosmos contains three such species: C_1s, C_2s, and C_3s. Without using the direct theological words, Percy lets us discover that C_1s are innocent, unfallen, and harmless; C_2s are fallen—alienated from themselves, God, each other, and nature, and prone to selfishness, competition, and violence; and C_3s are C_2s who have known themselves, become aware of their predicament, and "asked for help" (i.e., repented). The Alpha Centaurians determine, through a few significant, probing questions (especially about sexual behavior), that earthlings are not C_1s. They ask them, "Have you asked for help?" The earthlings have no idea what that could mean. Then the Alpha Centaurians realize that the earthlings are C_2s, not C_3s. Permission to land is denied. The last humans die in orbit. Man is abolished. The carbuncle on the cosmos is removed.

Why do I call this story optimistic? Because there is another possible ending. All that C2s have to do is to admit that they are C2s, and they become C3s. But to do that, to repent, they must believe in a real moral law, at least, if not a God, to repent to. That is why denying the natural law is such a radical step. Such a denial will lead, either spiritually or physically, to the abolition of man.

The obstacle to salvation is not sin. It is impenitence. The road to Hell is not paved with good intentions (what a stupid saying!), or even with evil intentions, but with impenitence, shamelessness, pop psychology, self-help. The only people the Savior *didn't* come to save are those people who think they *aren't* lost. "I came not to call the righteous, but sinners, to repentence." Jesus came not for C1s or for C2s who think they're C1s, but for C3s, like Dr. Tom More. What the Christian spy Percy smuggles in to the fortress of the secular modern mentality under cover of fiction and satire is the thing modernity most vehemently hates and fears: the notion of sin. For modernity the only sin is to believe in sin.

The road from being "lost in the cosmos" to being "abolished" is not an inevitable slide. We are on that road now, but we can turn back. Lewis and Percy say the same thing all the prophets say.

But to turn back, we must admit we are headed in the wrong direction. Pascal says that there are only two kinds of people in the world: saints who know they are sinners, and sinners who think they are saints. In other words, C3s and C2s. (There are no more C1s after Eden.)

Percy's and Lewis' "message in the bottle" is the first half of the gospel command to "repent and believe." Percy wrote not just to elicit laughs, and Lewis wrote not just to elicit thought, but both wrote to elicit repentence, the necessary preliminary to salvation.

If that worked on even one reader, it was worth all the books in the world.

6

The Joyful Cosmology:
Perelandra's "Great Dance" as an Alternative World View to Modern Reductionism

Of all the passages in all the over fifty books of my favorite author, C. S. Lewis, the "Great Dance" at the end of *Perelandra* is the one I have the most vivid and joy-filled memory of from my first reading, and the one I think I will most likely remember as I lie dying. When I first read it, I remember thinking, "This is too good to be true; this is 'good beyond hope' " (to use the phrase Lewis used to describe Tolkien's *The Lord of the Rings*). I had never read anything like it before, and I have not read anything like it since, except perhaps Lewis' own equally mystical description of the descent of the five planetary gods in *That Hideous Strength*. I didn't know at the time why it had such power over me. I think I know now. It was food for an empty stomach. Nature abhors a vacuum spiritually as well as physically.

The vacuum is the typically modern world view, which we could call the joyless cosmology. Lewis' is the joyful cosmology. We have all breathed that modern air, even those who disbelieve it or even despise it. Our lungs are full of reductionism, which is dead air. Then, suddenly, a gust of wet, salty air blows in from the sea, and our spirits spring up like children, full of mysterious joy. A smell from another country, a gleam of celestial beauty falling on our jungle of filth and imbecility (to use a formula from *Perelandra* itself). An angel, a heavenly messenger, a star. Ralph Waldo Emerson (I think) said: "If the stars should appear only one night in a thousand years, how mankind would wonder and be grateful for that vision of Heaven that had been shown!" Well, something like the "Great Dance" appears only once in a thousand books. That is why we appreciate it, as a Bedouin appreciates an oasis.

Put in a more scholarly way, we find here in poetic form a radical alternative to the dehumanizing world view that has starved and crushed our souls for centuries, especially this darkest of centuries.

One major cause of this darkness is ferreted out in *The Abolition of Man* as reductionism, only-ism, nothing-but-ism. Thought is only cerebral biochemistry, love is only lust, man is only a "trousered ape", religion is only myth, consciousness is only an epiphenomenon of matter, life is only the candle's brief and pointless sputter between two infinite expanses of darkness. The term Lewis uses for this view is Naturalism, the belief that nothing but Nature exists. Nature he defines on page 81 of *The Abolition of Man* as follows:

Nature is a word of varying meanings. . . .
1. Nature seems to be the spatial and temporal as distinct from what is less fully so or is not so at all [i.e., matter in the modern sense as distinct from the Greek, Aristotelian sense];
2. She seems to be the world of quantity as against the world of quality [i.e., matter in the Aristotelian sense as distinguished from forms or essences or Platonic Ideas];
3. of objects as against consciousness [for consciousness is supernatural in relation to the universe, since consciousness *knows* the universe, and 'the knowledge of a thing is not one of that thing's parts', as Lewis says in *Miracles;* therefore insofar as we know the universe, we transcend the universe];

4. of that which is bound as against the wholly or partly autonomous [for freedom follows consciousness as will follows intellect; the degree of consciousness is also the degree of freedom];

5. of that which knows no values as against that which both has and perceives value [for values transcend facts, the 'ought' cannot be derived simply from the 'is', as Lewis showed in part 2 of *The Abolition of Man* and as G. E. Moore proved logically in *Principia Ethica* — value too is supernatural];

6. of efficient causes — or, in some modern systems, of no causality at all — as against final causes [i.e., purposes, ends; therefore nature is also the realm of *kronos*-time, which measures matter but not mind or purpose, as distinct from *kairos*-time, time *for* something, time that measures mind].

All of these points are connected. For instance, *kronos*-time is quantitative: it is seconds or light-years; but *kairos*-time is qualitative: it is time for this rather than that. "End" has a double meaning, like "time": the quantitative end point in a process and the meaning or purpose of the process. In the first sense, the end of life is death; in the second sense, the end of life is love.

Lewis then goes on:

When we [1] understand a thing analytically and then [2] dominate it and use it for our own convenience, we reduce it to the level of 'nature' in the sense that we suspend our judgements of value about it, ignore its final cause . . . and treat it in terms of quantity. This repression of elements in what would otherwise be our total reaction to it is sometimes very noticeable and even painful: something has to be overcome before we can cut up a dead man or a live animal in a dissecting room. These objects resist the [reductionistic] movement of the mind whereby we thrust them into the world of mere nature.

Notice that our natural, normal, instinctive, prescientific consciousness of and reaction to things is fuller, more adequate to the whole thing, more objective, more revelatory of the object's own total being, than our later, more precise and analytical abstractions.

Thus, as Heidegger startlingly says, poetry may be more objective than science.

Lewis concludes with a vision of two sciences, reductionistic versus nonreductionistic:

> It is not the greatest of modern scientists who feel most sure that the object, stripped of its qualitative properties and reduced to mere quantity, is wholly real.... The great minds know well that the object, so treated, is an artificial abstraction, that something of its reality has been lost....
>
> Nothing I can say will prevent some people from describing this lecture as an attack on science. I deny the charge, of course. But I can go further than that. I even suggest that from Science herself the cure might come.... Is it possible to imagine a new natural philosophy [cosmology] continually conscious that the 'natural object' produced by analysis and abstraction is not reality but only a view, and always correcting the abstraction?

Lewis wrote that in 1947. He could not have foreseen the remarkable developments in physics since then that have led some to say that matter behaves more like mind than like anything else we know, or the breakdown of the classical mechanistic physics that was still a formidable and slayable dragon in his day. Nor could he have foreseen that Kuhn's thesis about paradigms and paradigm shifts and horizons would come to dominate the new philosophy of science—a thesis in some ways similar to his own point about "views" quoted here and put more fully in *The Discarded Image.*

(I think Kuhn and Lewis are not saying the same thing, however. Lewis is more of a Platonist or an Aristotelian, while Kuhn is more of a Kantian. The "Copernican Revolution in philosophy" stands between these two. Yet both are freed from the reductionism which we have learned from the theologians to call "demythologizing".)

Perelandra is a remythologizing. The cosmology of all three books in the "space trilogy" is Lewis' poetic and fictional but serious attempt to contribute to the "new natural philosophy" or anti-reductionistic cosmology that he called for in *The Abolition of Man.* We need poets and novelists as well as scientists and philosophers of science to help build the new joyful cosmology, and I know of none, except perhaps Tolkien, who has contributed more to the building of this cathedral than Lewis—especially in his fiction, more especially in the "space trilogy", still more especially in *Perelandra,* and most especially in the "Cosmic Dance"—to which we now turn, having seen its historical and cosmological importance.

Perelandra is a novel of conflict, of *jihad,* of spiritual warfare. So is *That Hideous Strength.* Both books resemble the Apocalypse. There is a ubiquitous dualism: for every good, an evil; for every evil, a good. For evil is good bent. The spiritual conflict in the Green Lady's soul, fed by the verbal and later physical conflict between Ransom and Weston, is parallel to the philosophical conflict between two world views, Weston's nihilistic reductionism and Ransom's Christianity, Weston's demythologized cosmology and Ransom's (Lewis') remythologized cosmology that Ransom learns—*sees,* in fact—from the eldila (= angels) in the "Great Dance". We therefore need to look carefully at three passages:

1. the identification of the philosophical enemy to be slain by the joyful cosmology, which Lewis calls "the Empirical Bogey";

2. the eldila who teach it and who are a central part of it, Mars and Venus, the cosmic Masculine and Feminine; and

3. the "Great Dance" itself.

The "Empirical Bogey"

When Ransom first traveled through outer space in *Out of the Silent Planet,* he was amazed and delighted to see for himself—to see concretely, with his eyes, not just abstractly, with his mind—that the cosmology of emptiness and nihilism was false:

> Ransom, as time wore on, became aware of another and more spiritual cause for his progressive lightening and exultation of heart. A nightmare, long engendered in the modern mind by the mythology that follows in the wake of science, was falling off him. He had read of 'Space'; at the back of his thinking for years had lurked the dismal fancy of the black, cold vacuity, the utter deadness, which was supposed to separate the worlds. He had not known how much it affected him till now—now that the very name 'Space' seemed a blasphemous libel for this empyrean ocean of radiance in which they swam. He could not call it 'dead'; he felt life pouring into him from it every moment. How indeed should it be otherwise, since out of this ocean the worlds and all their life had come? He had thought it barren; he saw now that it was the womb of worlds, whose blazing and innumerable offspring looked down nightly even upon the earth with so many eyes—and here, with how many more! No; Space was the wrong name. Older thinkers had been wiser when they named it simply the heavens. . . .

This is recalled in *Perelandra* (p. 164) when it is threatened by the world view of Weston—i.e., the modern West—from which we need to be saved, or Ransomed:

> In vain did Ransom try to remember that he had been in 'space' and found it Heaven, tingling with a fulness of life for which infinity itself was not one cubic inch too large. All that seemed like a dream. That opposite mode of thought which he had often mocked and called in mockery The Empirical Bogey, came surging into his mind—the great myth of our century with its gases and galaxies, its light years and evolutions, its nightmare perspectives of simple arithmetic in which everything that can possibly hold significance for the mind becomes the mere by-product of essential disorder.

The practical consequences of this theoretical picture, the life view that follows from this world view, is literally deadly to the soul. Thus it needs a Ransom, a Savior, for this view of life has its origin and end in Hell. Weston says:

'That's why it's so important to live as long as you can. All the good things are now—a thin little rind of what we call life, put on for show, and then—the *real* universe for ever and ever. To thicken the rind by one centimetre—to live one week, one day, one half-hour longer—that's the only thing that matters. . . . That's all there is to us (pp. 168–69).'

Ransom replies to Weston with Lewis' favorite argument:

'That could hardly be the whole story. . . . If the whole universe were like that, then we, being parts of it, would feel at home in such a universe. The very fact that it strikes us as monstrous—'

'Yes,' interrupted Weston, 'that would be all very well if it wasn't that reasoning itself is only valid as long as you stay in the rind. It has nothing to do with the real universe. . . . [R]eality is neither rational nor consistent nor anything else. In a sense you might say it isn't there. "Real" and "Unreal," "true" and "false"—they're all only on the surface. They give way the moment you press them.'

'If all this were true,' said Ransom, 'what would be the point of saying it?'

'Or of anything else?' replied Weston. 'The only point in anything is that there isn't any point.'

Sound familiar? It is a frighteningly accurate prophecy of the philosophy regnant today among sophisticated intellectuals, namely, post-modernism, or Deconstructionism. (I must spit out the word in disgust as a good Muslim spits out the word "al-co-hol".) Sartre's Roquentin, in *Nausea,* and Camus' Meursault, in *The Stranger,* live this philosophy. It is the death of the soul. It is Hell. (Hell is not where souls go to live forever; that's Heaven. Hell is where souls go to die forever. See Matthew 10:28.)

We need to be ransomed from sin, but we also need to be

ransomed from this philosophy, Hell's cosmology, the logical consequence of reductionism.

Bertrand Russell saw those logical consequences and put them brilliantly in the famous passage from "A Free Man's Worship":

> Such ... is the world which Science presents for our belief. Amid such a world, if anywhere, our ideals henceforward must find a home. That Man is the product of causes which had no prevision of the end they were achieving; that his origin, his growth, his hopes and fears, his loves and his beliefs, are but the outcome of accidental collocations of atoms; that no fire, no heroism, no intensity of thought and feeling, can preserve an individual life beyond the grave; that all the labours of the ages, all the devotion, all the inspiration, all the noonday brightness of human genius, are destined to extinction in the vast death of the solar system, and that the whole temple of Man's achievement must inevitably be buried beneath the debris of a universe in ruins—all these things, if not quite beyond dispute, are yet so nearly certain that no philosophy which rejects them can hope to stand. Only within the scaffolding of these truths, only on the firm foundation of unyielding despair, can the soul's habitation henceforth be safely built.

This is a philosophy but it is also a spell, a spell of black magic laid on the human soul. Philosophical arguments are needed to refute the philosophy, but philosophical arguments alone will not lift the spell. Only a counterspell will. Only good magic defeats bad magic. We need a spell weaver, a magician. When Tolkien's son had to fill out a draft induction form, he filled in the blank for "father's occupation" with the word "wizard". The same could be said for Lewis, especially in *Perelandra*.

Two of the greatest questions we need the true answers to are: What are we? and What is the universe? Myths gave us answers to these two questions for most of our history on this planet, until they dried up and left the desert of demythologized reductionism. Two of the most widespread myths that answered these two questions were: the myth of Mars and Venus, or Yang and Yin, or cosmic Masculine and Feminine, which told us who we are; and the myth of the "Cosmic Dance", which showed us what the universe is. Lewis rehabilitates or resurrects these precious myths for us in a Christianized but not demythologized form. For he learned from Tolkien that "the Gospel did not abrogate myths, but hallowed them" ("On Fairy Stories"). In fact, the gospel, says Lewis, is "myth become fact".

Cosmic Masculine and Feminine

This is a notion that is present in nearly every culture throughout time and space except our own. That fact must contribute to the rampant sexual confusion and decadence that also differentiate our culture sharply and spectacularly. For how can sex be sacred unless it is cosmic?

In late Greek philosophy, *angels* and Platonic Forms, or *essences,* were sometimes confused or identified, since both were eternal, perfect, and immaterial. It is therefore appropriate that the essential meaning or archetypal Idea of the masculine and feminine be revealed in *Perelandra* by angels (eldils).

In my opinion, there are two things Lewis describes better than anyone who has ever written: *Sehnsucht* and angels. That is my justification for the following rather lengthy quotation, interspersed with comment and interpretation, like a Christmas tree festooned with decorations. Another justification is the intrinsic and contemporary importance of the question of sex and gender.

The eldils of *Perelandra* make three attempts to appear to the human consciousness of Ransom. The first two, though unsuccessful, are almost as fascinating as the third, which remains:

> A tornado of sheer monstrosities seemed to be pouring over Ransom. Darting pillars filled with eyes, lightning pulsations

of flame, talons and beaks and billowy masses of what suggested snow, volleyed through cubes and heptagons into an infinite black void. 'Stop it . . . stop it,' he yelled, and the scene cleared. He . . . gave the eldila to understand that this kind of appearance was not suited to human sensations. 'Look then at this,' said the voices again. And he looked with some reluctance, and far off between the peaks on the other side of the little valley there came rolling wheels. There was nothing but that—concentric wheels moving with a rather sickening slowness one inside the other. There was nothing terrible about them if you could get used to their appalling size, but there was also nothing significant. He bade them to try yet a third time. And suddenly two human figures stood before him.

They were perhaps thirty feet high. They were burning white like white-hot iron. The outline of their bodies when he looked at it steadily against the red landscape seemed to be faintly, swiftly undulating as though the permanence of their shape, like that of waterfalls or flames, co-existed with a rushing movement of the matter it contained. . . .

Whenever he looked straight at them they appeared to be rushing towards him with enormous speed. . . . This may have been due in part to the fact that their long and sparkling hair stood out straight behind them as if in a great wind. . . . They were not standing quite vertically in relation to the floor of the valley: but to Ransom it appeared (as it had appeared to me on Earth when I saw one) that the eldils were vertical. It was the valley—it was the whole world of Perelandra—which was aslant (p. 198).

This is good relativity theory. The whole universe is relative to the observer, matter to spirit, nature to that which observes and thus transcends nature. Planets are relative to angels, not vice versa.

"He remembered the words of Oyarsa long ago in Mars, 'I am not *here* in the same way you are *here*.'"

This is good angelology too, Aquinas would say.

He told me he could in a sense remember the colours—that is, he would know them if he ever saw them again—but that he cannot by any effort call up a visual image of them nor give them any name. The very few people with whom he and I can discuss these matters all give the same explanation. We think that when creatures of the hypersomatic kind choose to "appear" to us, they are not in fact affecting our retina at all, but directly manipulating the relevant parts of our brain. If so, it is quite possible that they can produce there the sensations we *should* have if our eyes were capable of receiving those colours in the spectrum which are actually beyond their range.

The 'plumage' or halo of the one eldil was extremely different from that of the other. The Oyarsa of Mars shone with cold and morning colours, a little metallic—pure, hard, and bracing. The Oyarsa of Venus glowed with a warm splendour, full of the suggestion of teeming vegetable life (p. 199).

Hard versus soft, tough versus gentle—we need both.

The faces surprised him very much. Nothing less like the 'angel' of popular art could well be imagined. The rich variety, the hint of undeveloped possibilities, which make the interest of human faces, were entirely absent. [They are eternal Platonic archetypes.] One single, changeless expression—so clear that it hurt and dazzled him—was stamped on each and there was nothing else there at all. In that sense their faces were as 'primitive,' as unnatural, if you like, as those of archaic statues from Aegina. [Were those statues based on real angels that were seen? We wonder.] What this one thing was he could not be certain. He concluded in the end that it was charity. [The essential nature or core of love.] But it was terrifyingly different from the expression of human charity, which we always see either blossoming out of, or hastening to descend into, natural affection. Here there was no affection at all: no least lingering memory of it even at ten million years' distance, no germ from which it could spring in any future, however remote. Pure, spiritual, intellectual love shot from their faces like barbed lightning. It was so unlike the love we experience that its expression could easily be mistaken for ferocity (pp. 199–200).

The reader who finds this incomprehensible simply does not understand the essence of love as distinct from its affectionate accidents. Perhaps the biblical "wrath of God" is explainable as this very thing: pure charity experienced by those whom it tortures rather than fulfills.

> Both the bodies were naked, and both were free from any sexual characteristics, either primary or secondary. That, one would have expected. But whence came this curious difference between them? He found that he could point to no single feature wherein the difference resided, yet it was impossible to ignore. One could try—Ransom tried a hundred times—to put it into words. He has said that Malacandra was like rhythm and Perelandra like melody (p. 200).

Another universal and cross-cultural analogy. "I am the sun, you are the moon; I am the words, you are the tune."

"He thinks that the first held in his hand something like a spear, but the hands of the other were open, with the palms towards him. . . ."

The sexual symbolism is obvious. But it is not *allegory.* The spear is not an allegory for the penis, nor the open palms for the womb. Rather, both things are expressions of the same spiritual Platonic archetype.

> What Ransom saw at that moment was the real meaning of gender. Everyone must sometimes have wondered why in nearly all tongues certain inanimate objects are masculine and others feminine. What is masculine about a mountain or feminine about certain trees? Ransom has cured me of believing that this is a purely morphological phenomenon, depending on the form of the word. Still less is gender an imaginative extension of sex. Our ancestors did not make mountains masculine because they projected male characteristics into them. The real process is the reverse. Gender is a reality, and a more fundamental reality than sex. Sex is, in fact, merely the adaption to organic life of a fundamental polarity which divides all created beings. Female sex is simply one of the things that have feminine

gender; there are many others, and Masculine and Feminine meet us on planes of reality where male and female would be simply meaningless . . . (p. 200).

Lewis uses the words "gender" and "sex" in the old sense, not the new attenuated sense in which "gender" means not cosmic Masculine and Feminine but simply biological maleness or female-ness, and "sex" means not biological maleness and femaleness, but simply copulation, or any kind of sex organ arousal.

The remythologization here consists in restoring the fullness of reality to gender polarity, turning upside down the modern "projection" theory (because that is in fact upside down). It is similar to what Jesus does with the word "food" and what Saint Paul does with the word "Father" when Jesus says that doing God's will is real food, or "food indeed", not just a pale symbol for food (food is a pale symbol for it!), and when Paul says that all fatherhood and family on earth is named after the Father in Heaven, not vice versa.

Gender goes all the way down to positive and negative electri-cal charges, and all the way up into the angels, and perhaps even the Trinity. There is a parallel passage in *That Hideous Strength* where Jane discovers the principle Lewis states here and is converted, accepting God as her spiritual husband. The principle is just the reverse of Reductionism. Cosmic Masculine and Feminine are not a pale copy of biological male and female—exactly the reverse. Platonic Forms are not pale copies, by human minds, of material things; material things are pale copies of objective Platonic Ideas, eternal essences.

Masculine is not attenuated male, nor feminine attenuated female. On the contrary, the male and female of organic creatures are rather faint and blurred reflections of masculine and feminine. Their reproductive functions, their differences in strength and size, partly exhibit, but partly also confuse and misrepresent, the real polarity. All this Ransom saw, as it were, with his own eyes. The two white creatures were sexless. But he of Malacandra was masculine (not male); she of Perelandra was feminine (not female). Malacandra seemed to him to have the look of one standing armed at the ramparts of his own remote archaic world, in ceaseless vigilance, his eyes ever roaming the earth-ward horizon whence his danger came long ago. 'A sailor's look,' Ransom once said to me; 'you know . . . eyes that are impregnated with distance.' But the eyes of Perelandra opened, as it were, inward, as if they were the curtained gateway to a world of waves and murmurings and wandering airs, of life that rocked in winds and splashed on mossy stones and descended as the dew and arose sunward in thin-spun delicacy of mist. On Mars the very forests are of stone; in Venus the lands swim. . . . With deep wonder he thought to himself, 'My eyes have seen Mars and Venus. I have seen Ares and Aphrodite' (pp. 200–201).

Clearly this vision gives our ordinary empirical maleness and femaleness a far more momentous meaning, as a colony of a heavenly country. Such "supernatural sex" does not substitute for or lessen the significance or value of natural sex but vastly expands it.

The last question is the epistemological one: How do we on earth know these trans-earthly archetypes?

He asked them how they were known to the old poets of Tellus [earth]. . . . They told him, . . . 'There is an environment of minds as well as of space. The universe is one — a spider's web wherein each mind lives along every line, a vast whispering gallery where . . . no secret can be rigorously kept. . . . In the very matter of our world, the traces of the celestial commonwealth are not quite lost. Memory passes through the womb and hovers in the air. The Muse is a real thing. A faint breath, as Virgil says, reaches even the late generations. Our mythology is based on a solider reality than we dream; but it is also at an almost infinite distance from that base.' And when they told him this, Ransom at last understood why mythology was what it was — gleams of celestial strength and beauty falling on a jungle of filth and imbecility (p. 201).

Lewis is serious here. His explanation of myth is itself a myth. Myth, like science, explains data, explains experience. The myth of the cosmic whispering gallery, the unconscious telepathy with angels at a great distance, explains this strange twofold feature of earth's mythology: beauty and imbecility, their wisdom mixed with our folly.

There have been other deep thinkers who have also taken our earth's mythologies very seriously, e.g., Huston Smith (in *Forgotten Truth*), Mircea Eliade (in *The Sacred and the Profane*), and Fritjof Schuon (in *The Transcendent Unity of Religions*); but no one with Lewis' breadth, no one who was also a Christian apologist, Romantic poet, fantasy and science fiction novelist, and philosopher. He has not turned from all these things to mythology, but integrated mythology into them, or them into it. His mark always seems to be more, not less—Hamlet's philosophy that "there are more things in Heaven and earth, Horatio, than are dreamt of in your philosophies." The reductionist believes there are far *fewer* things in Heaven and earth, i.e., in objective reality, than in our philosophies, i.e., our minds; most of our ideas are myths in the pejorative sense. The rationalist and dogmatist believes that there are *the same number* of things in Heaven and earth (i.e., objective reality) as in his philosophy. The poet believes there are *more,* always more. Therefore the poet wonders, while the reductionist sneers and the dogmatist prattles.

The Cosmic Dance

The Dance is the culmination of the plot in *Perelandra* and, in fact, of the history of the universe. In visual and symbolic form, it is no less than the meaning of creation in a kind of cosmic choreography. It is a traditional image for a traditional idea, but Lewis uses it for a modern purpose: to combat the joyless cosmology with the joyful, to exorcise the demon of the Empirical Bogey, the empty and meaningless universe conjured up by the black magic of reductionism. Here, in poetic and mythic form, is the world view of the new non-reductionistic science that Lewis himself called for in *The Abolition of Man.*

It is, first of all, a *dance.* Play, Lewis says in *Letters to Malcolm,* is more ultimate, more heavenly, than work. It is its own end, not an instrumental means to a further end. "The serious business of Heaven is joy." Thus it is called "The Great *Game*".

The cosmic *setting* of this play, or game, or dance, is the remythologized universe, freed from the Empirical Bogey (which we saw in part 1). The archetypal *characters* of the play are Mars and Venus, cosmic Masculine and Feminine (which we saw in part 2). The *plot* is the Great Dance. We are now ready to review the plot, and in it the *theme:* What is the point, the "center" of it all?

We are privileged to see (or hear) this from an angel's eye viewpoint.

"The speeches followed one another—if, indeed, they did not all take place at the same time—like the parts of a music into which all five of them had entered as instruments." Music is more fundamental than speech. The language of Heaven is music.

> 'The Great Dance does not wait to be perfect until the peoples of the Low Worlds [the solar system] are gathered into it. We speak not of when it will begin. It has begun from before always. [This is the angelic point of view, transcending material time.] There was no time when we did not rejoice before His face as now. The dance which we dance is at the centre and for the dance all things were made. Blessed be He!' (p. 214).

The question is: What is at the center? What is the central meaning of all things? Is there anything at the center, or is everything relative? The first answer is that the whole dance, the dance as a whole, is at the center. The whole universe is at the center of the whole universe. For the universe, as a reflection of its Creator, is "an infinite sphere whose centre is everywhere and whose circumference is nowhere". For the dance all things were made, as for the play all things in the play are made: the setting, the costumes, the stage, the syllables. The singer is for the song, not the song for the singer.

> Another said, 'Never did He make two things the same; never did He utter one word twice. After earths, not better earths but beasts; after beasts, not better beasts, but spirits. After a falling, not a recovery but a new creation. Out of the new creation, not a third but the mode of change itself is changed for ever. Blessed be He!'

Creation, physical evolution, biological evolution, redemption, and the afterlife are five different *modes* of change, like five different temporal *dimensions.*

> Another said, 'It is loaded with justice as a tree bows down with fruit. All is righteousness and there is no equality. [Natural or cosmic justice is inequality; human or political justice is equality. How provincial to project our fallen little justice onto the universe, as if the stars needed to wear the same clothes that protect us against the consequences of our Fall!] Not as when stones lie side by side, but as when stones support and are supported in an arch, such is His order [like the human body, not like an army marching]: rule and obedience [two modernly unpopular words!], begetting and bearing [increasingly ditto!], heat glancing down, life growing up. Blessed be He!' (p. 214).

All great ancient societies (Greek, Chinese, Hindu) knew that justice was like music: not unison but harmony. Uniforms and uniformity and equality suggest a totalitarian mindset rather than a natural one—one appropriate to our century. The social consequences of cosmological models are immense.

> One said, 'They who add years to years in lumpish aggregation, or miles to miles and galaxies to galaxies, shall not come near His greatness. [Quantity—the language of computers and exact science—is not the language of Heaven, or of nature]. . . . Not thus is He great. He dwells (all of Him dwells) within the seed of the smallest flower and is not cramped; Deep Heaven is inside Him who is inside the seed and does not distend Him. Blessed be He!' (pp. 214–15).

Our modern model is simply inside out and upside down when we prioritize quantity over quality, matter over spirit.

> 'The edge of each nature borders on that whereof it contains no shadow or similitude. Of many points, one line; of many lines one shape; of many shapes one solid body; of many senses and thoughts one person; of three persons, Himself' (p. 215).

Here Lewis takes the traditional medieval idea of the Great Chain of Being and puts it into the more abstract and philosophically sophisticated form of *dimensions.* His essay on dimensions, "Transformation", in *The Weight of Glory and Other Addresses,* is, I think, the most philosophically original and suggestive thing he ever wrote.

> 'The peoples of the ancient worlds who never sinned, for whom He never came down, are the peoples for whose sake the Low Worlds were made. For though the healing what was wounded and the straightening what was bent is a new dimension of glory [the *felix culpa*], yet the straight was not made that it might be bent nor the whole that it might be wounded. The ancient [unfallen] peoples are at the centre. Blessed be He!' (p. 215).

Better is innocence than repentence. Better would we have been if our ancestors had not fallen. Better are we even now when we avoid sin than when we sin and then repent. Better are those extraterrestrial races, if they exist, which have not sinned (and God preserve them from our space ships!).

Lewis says, by the way, that one useful way of expressing the doctrine of the Fall and of free will and responsibility is that if there are other races of intelligent beings on other worlds, it is not necessary to suppose that they have sinned. A useful "disputed question" for the theologians; why have none picked it up, I wonder?

> 'In the Fallen World He prepared for Himself a body and was united with the Dust and made it glorious for ever. This is the

end and final cause of all creating, and the sin whereby it came is called Fortunate and the world where this was enacted is the centre of all worlds. Blessed be He!' (p. 215).

Earth is the dramatic center of the universe, though not the physical center. For here is the stage where the Creator came down to play the central part in his own play. God came into the universe as a man, not a Martian. All other unfallen races that know God must long to make pilgrimages to our ironically privileged planet. Perhaps they do, invisibly. A corking good story could be made out of that idea.

'Though men or angels rule them, the worlds are for themselves. The waters you have not floated on, the fruit you have not plucked, the caves into which you have not descended and the fire through which your bodies cannot pass, do not await your coming to put on perfection, though they will obey you when you come. Times without number I [either Mars or Venus] have circled Arbol [Sol] while you were not alive, and those times were not desert. Their own voice was in them, not merely a dreaming of the day when you should awake. They also were at the centre. Be comforted, small immortals. You are not the voice that all things utter, nor is there eternal silence in the places where you cannot come. No feet have walked, nor shall, on the ice of Glund; no eye looked up from beneath on the Ring of Lurga, and Iron-plain in Neruval is chaste and empty. Yet it is not for nothing that the gods walk ceaselessly around the fields of Arbol. Blessed be He!' (pp. 215–16).

Now this is hard to take. Anthropocentrism and subjectivism and pride have so deeply infected even us Christians that we are shocked by this absence of "humanism". Though we are at the center, we are not the center. Man is not God. That simple formula should suffice to refute humanism. And once we are done with humanism, what a breeze of relief! We can let beings be. We don't have to think the Ring of Lurga is a contrived lesson for us from God, or a mere opportunity for us to make something out of it, but can be wonderfully wild and free to be itself. We are little children in the Father's enormous and mysterious house. We are not the Master. We can play.

> 'That Dust itself, which is scattered so rare in Heaven, whereof all worlds, and the bodies that are not worlds, are made, is at the centre. . . . Only the least part has served, or ever shall, a beast (or) a man. . . . But . . . it is what it is and utters the heart of the Holy One with its own voice. It is farthest from Him of all things, for it has no life, nor sense, nor reason; it is nearest to Him of all things for without intervening soul, as sparks fly out of fire, He utters in each grain of it the unmixed image of His energy. Each grain, if it spoke, would say, I am at the centre; for me all things were made. Let no mouth open to gainsay it. Blessed be He!' (p. 216).

Even matter is at the center, because it is innocent and pure, because it hosts God's presence, and simply because it *is*.

What, then, is the center? What is the absolute within the universe? What is the answer to the sickening feeling in the stomach that we get when we realize that Einstein is right and we are on sea, not on land? Where is the solid ground? Where is the navel of the cosmos, so that we can stick into it the tent pole of our temple, as the primitive peoples were wont to do? The answer is: everything and nothing. Everything, because of the divine immanence; nothing, because of the divine transcendence.

> 'Where Maleldil is, there is the centre. He is in every place. [Ergo . . . every place is the center.] Not some of Him in one place and some in another, but in each place the whole Maleldil, even in the smallness beyond thought. There is no way out of the centre save into the Bent Will which casts itself into the Nowhere. Blessed be He!' (p. 216).

The nature of the true center, God, accounts for the fact that the center is everywhere. For God is not a finite creature with a finite essence; therefore he does not displace other creatures or essences, or contest place with them. His very transcendence allows him to be totally immanent everywhere, as the transcendence of light over any color (light is no color) allows light to light up and perfect *all* colors, or as the transcendence of mind over matter (for "the knowledge of a thing is not one of that thing's parts") allows mind to know and be present to all matter—and God to all minds.

> 'Each thing was made for Him. [Saint Paul claims this for Christ in Colossians 1:16.] He is the centre. Because we are with him, each of us is at the centre. [The only true humanism!] It is not as in a city of the Darkened World where they say that each must live for all. In His city all things are made for each. When He died in the Wounded World He died not for men, but for each man. If each man had been the only man made, He would have done no less' (pp. 216–17).

A thrilling and humbling thought: Christ died not for "mankind", but for *me.* There are no abstractions with God.

> 'He has immeasurable use for each thing that is made, that His love and splendour may flow forth like a strong river which has need of a great watercourse and fills alike the deep pools and the little crannies, that are filled equally and remain unequal; and when it has filled them brim full it flows over and makes new channels. We also have need beyond measure of all that He has made. Love me, my brothers, for I am infinitely necessary to you and for your delight I was made. Blessed be He!' (p. 217).
>
> 'He has no need at all of anything that is made. An eldil is not more needful to Him than a grain of the Dust . . . and what all add to Him is nothing. We also have no need of anything that is made. Love me, my brothers, for I am infinitely superfluous, and your love shall be like His, born neither of your need nor of my deserving, but a plain bounty. Blessed be He!' (p. 217).

Here is the nature of *agape,* the nature of God: the paradox of infinite use and no need. If we realized and practiced this vision on earth, that would be the Kingdom, that would be his will being done on earth as it is in Heaven.

And now, by a transition which he did not notice, it seemed that what had begun as speech was turned into sight, or into something that can be remembered only as if it were seeing. He thought he saw the Great Dance. It seemed to be woven out of the intertwining undulation of many cords or bands of light, leaping over and under one another and mutually embraced in arabesques and flower-like subtleties. Each figure as he looked at it became the master-figure or focus of the whole spectacle, by means of which his eye disentangled all else and brought it into unity — only to be itself entangled when he looked to what he had taken for mere marginal decorations and found that there also the same hegemony was claimed, and the claim made good, yet the former pattern not thereby dispossessed but finding in its new subordination a significance greater than that which it had abdicated. He could see also (but the word 'seeing' is now plainly inadequate) wherever the ribbons or serpents of light intersected, minute corpuscles of momentary brightness: and he knew somehow that these particles were the secular generalities of which history tells — peoples, institutions, climates of opinion, civilisations, arts, sciences, and the like — ephemeral coruscations that piped their short song and vanished. The ribbons or cords themselves, in which millions of corpuscles lived and died, were things of some different kind. At first he could not say what. But he knew in the end that most of them were individual entities (pp. 218–19).

This passage will conjure up, to the mind of everyone who has read it, the great paragraph at the end of *The Weight of Glory:* "You have never talked to a mere mortal. Nations, cultures, arts, civilisations — these are mortal, and their life is to ours as the life of a gnat. But it is immortals whom we joke with, work with, marry, snub, and exploit — immortal horrors or everlasting splendours."

But not all the cords were individuals: some were universal truths or universal qualities. It did not surprise him then to find that these and the persons were both cords and both stood together as against the mere atoms of generality which lived and died in the clashing of their streams: but afterwards, when he came back to earth, he wondered (p. 219).

Of course Truth and Goodness and Beauty are immortal and so are Sam and Kate and Susie, but not democracy or Humanism or Post-impressionism.

> And by now the thing must have passed altogether out of the region of sight as we understand it . . . as dimension was added to dimension and that part of him which could reason and remember was dropped farther and farther behind that part of him which saw, even then, at the very zenith of complexity, complexity was eaten up and faded, as a thin white cloud fades into the hard blue burning of the sky, and a simplicity beyond all comprehension, ancient and young as spring, illimitable, pellucid, drew him with cords of infinite desire into its own stillness. He went up into such a quietness, a privacy, and a freshness that at the very moment when he stood farthest from our ordinary mode of being he had the sense of stripping off encumbrances and awaking from trance, and coming to himself. With a gesture of relaxation he looked about him . . . (p. 219).

This last, mystical paragraph strongly resembles the accounts of many authentic mystics, both Eastern and Western (for one would expect the human spirit not to change when we travel East; to be deprived of true theology is not to be deprived of one's own human nature). It also resembles Lewis' account of his conversion in *Surprised by Joy,* where he uses the same image of stripping off encumbrances, or clothing, or armor, like a snakeskin. Finally, it resembles the end of *A Grief Observed,* where he records the simplicity and nonemotionality of the intimacy with which he experienced the presence of his dead wife, and especially the final conclusion in the final paragraph, which speaks so wonderfully teasingly of "that impression which I can't describe except by saying that it's like the sound of a chuckle in the darkness. The sense that some shattering and disarming simplicity is the real answer."

Chesterton knew the same secret, and he learned it from the same Source as Lewis. The Source is Christ and the secret is his laughter:

Joy, which was the small publicity of the pagan, is the gigantic secret of the Christian. . . . The tremendous figure which fills the Gospels towers in this respect, as in every other, above all the thinkers. . . . The Stoics, ancient and modern, were proud of concealing their tears. He never concealed His tears. . . . Yet He concealed something. Solemn supermen and imperial diplomatists are proud of restraining their anger. He never restrained His anger. He flung furniture down the front steps of the Temple and asked men how they expected to escape the damnation of Hell. Yet He restrained something. I say it with reverence: there was in that shattering personality a thread that must be called shyness. There was something that He hid from all men when He went up a mountain to pray. . . . There was some one thing that was too great for God to show us when He walked upon our earth; and I have sometimes fancied that it was His mirth (*Orthodoxy*).

This is the wardrobe into Narnia. This is the door out of our agonized world of spiritual darkness "where ignorant armies clash by night". This is the joy the New Testament speaks of in the strangest way anyone has ever spoken of joy. It is the joy of Christ, that came in the most unlikely place and time in all of history, Calvary. It is the secret of "him who for the *joy* that was set before him endured the cross, despising the shame, and is seated at the right hand of the throne of God" (Heb 12:2). This is the joy that conquered Hell on the Cross; the joy that was the door Christ saw behind the Cross, the cross-shaped door whose other side is a crown; the death-shaped mask worn by the Lord of life.

The only adequate answer to our "century of genocide", and the triumph of the principalities and powers of wickedness in heavenly places, and the threat of the Brave New World, and the abolition of man, is the secret that frees us into this "gesture of relaxation" that is the culmination of the Great Dance: the smile on the face of God.

CONCLUSION

Optimism or pessimism about the third millennium? We have no crystal ball, but we have clues. What is the bottom line? The bottom line is optimism.

Why? Because apocalyptically decadent ages elicit saints. Suffering elicits courage, compassion, heroism, and martyrdom. Evil elicits good in response. Bad times make good people, as mountainous pressures make diamonds or as fire tempers steel.

We should have great hopes for America. For if she emerges from her present crisis she will be stronger than ever before. Defeating British economic tyranny in the Revolutionary War gave us only political independence. Defeating slavery in the Civil War gave us only personal freedom for all. Defeating Fascist totalitarianism in World War II gave us only a "free world". But defeating moral decadence and confusion would give us moral strength and clarity, perhaps even holiness. Perhaps the next millennium could even issue in *the* Millennium of Revelation 20. For the more dangerous the enemy, the more precious the victory.

Therefore the twenty-first century will be one of two things. Either it will be the best since the thirteenth, or the worst since the twenty-first B.C., before the Call of Abraham and the founding of Judaism. It depends on which side wins the current war. Either we will build Gothic cathedrals again, from a restored faith, or we will build the Tower of Babel again, from a restored apostasy.

Lewis, like all prophets, gives us the road map, the clear choice between the two roads of life or death, and the Mosaic simplicity of the challenge to "choose life".

Please do. Please help save the world. Please be a saint.

BIBLIOGRAPHY

The following is a list of books and articles by C. S. Lewis referred to in this book. In many cases there are a number of editions available.

The Abolition of Man, or, Reflections on Education with Special Reference to the Teaching of English in the Upper Forms of Schools. Riddell Memorial Lectures, Fifteenth Series. Oxford: Oxford University Press, 1943; London: G. Bles, 1946; New York: Macmillan, 1947.

The Allegory of Love: A Study in Medieval Tradition. New York: Oxford, 1936.

"A Cliché Came out of Its Cage". In *Poems* (see below). Earlier version published in *Nine: A Magazine of Poetry and Criticism,* May 1950.

"De Descriptione Temporum". Published in *They Asked for a Paper: Papers and Addresses.* London: G. Bles, 1962.

The Discarded Image: An Introduction to Medieval and Renaissance Literature. Cambridge: Cambridge University Press, 1964.

English Literature in the Sixteenth Century. Oxford History of English Literature, vol. 3. Oxford: Clarendon, 1954.

An Experiment in Criticism. Cambridge: Cambridge University Press, 1961.

"First and Second Things" first published as "Notes on the Way" from *Time and Tide,* vol. 23 (June 27, 1942). Reprinted in *God in the Dock,* see below.

The Four Loves. G. Bles, 1960; New York: Harcourt, Brace and World, 1960.

God in the Dock: Essays on Theology and Ethics. Edited by Walter Hooper. Grand Rapids, Michigan: William B. Eerdmans, 1970.

A Grief Observed. Published under the pseudonym N. W. Clerk. London: Faber and Faber, 1961; reprinted as by C. S. Lewis, 1964.

The Last Battle: A Story for Children. London: G. Bles, 1950; New York: Macmillan, 1950, 1962.

The Lion, the Witch, and the Wardrobe: A Story for Children. London: The Bodley Head, 1950; New York: Macmillan, 1956, 1962.

Letters of C. S. Lewis, ed. W. H. Lewis. New York: Harcourt Brace and World, 1975.

Mere Christianity: A revised and enlarged edition, with a new introduction, of the three books 'The Case for Christianity', 'Christian Behavior', and 'Beyond Personality'. London: G. Bles, 1952; New York: Macmillan, 1952.

Miracles: A Preliminary Study. G. Bles, 1947; New York: Macmillan, 1947.

Perelandra. John Lane, 1943; New York: Macmillan, 1947.

The Pilgrim's Regress: An Allegorical Apology for Christianity, Reason and Romanticism. J. M. Dent, 1933; Sheed and Ward, 1935; Grand Rapids, Michigan: Eerdmans, 1958.

Poems, edited by Walter Hooper. G. Bles, 1964; Harcourt, Brace and World, 1965.

A Preface to 'Paradise Lost': Being the Ballard Matthews Lectures Delivered at University College, North Wales, 1941. Revised and enlarged. London: Oxford University Press, 1942.

Prince Caspian: The Return to Narnia. London: G. Bles, 1951; New York: Macmillan, 1951, 1962.

The Problem of Pain. London: G. Bles, 1940. New York: Macmillan, 1943.

Reflections on the Psalms. London: G. Bles, 1958; New York: Harcourt, Brace and World, 1958.

The Screwtape Letters. London: G. Bles, 1942; New York: Macmillan, 1943. *The Screwtape Letters and Screwtape Proposes a Toast.* New York: Macmillan, 1961.

Surprised by Joy: The Shape of My Early Life. G. Bles, 1955; New York: Harcourt, Brace and World, 1956.

That Hideous Strength: A Modern Fairy-Tale for Grown-ups. John Lane, 1945; New York: Macmillan, 1946.

Till We Have Faces: A Myth Retold. Geoffrey Bles, 1956. New York: Harcourt, Brace and World, 1957; London: Collins, Son, and Company, 1979.

The Weight of Glory and Other Addresses. Revised and expanded edition, edited with an introduction by Walter Hooper. New York: Macmillan, 1980.

For a more complete bibliography of C. S. Lewis' writings, the reader is referred to the comprehensive bibliography compiled by Walter Hooper and published in *Light on C. S. Lewis* (New York: Harcourt, Brace and World, 1965), pages 117–48.